GOOD NEWS WITHOUT FEAR

How Jesus Reveals a God We Were Never Meant To Fear

John Faulkner

Copyright © 2026 John Faulkner

All rights reserved.

No part of this book may be reproduced or distributed in any form without written permission from the publisher, except for brief quotations in reviews.

ISBN: 978-0-646-73481-1

About the Author

John Faulkner writes at the intersection of faith, belonging, and quiet truth.

For more information, essays, and future books, visit:
https://johnfaulknerauthor.com

Contents

PREFACE 1

WHY THIS BOOK EXISTS 7

INTRODUCTION 11

DOCTRINAL MAP 30

SECTION I - SEEING CLEARLY AGAIN............................. 31

Chapter 1 — Jesus as the Final Revelation of God 32

Chapter 2 — The Doctrine of the Incarnation 35

Chapter 3 — How Scripture Is Meant to Be Read 40

Chapter 4 — God Revealed: Love Without Fear 44

SECTION II - WHAT WENT WRONG — AND WHAT WAS NEVER LOST... 47

Chapter 5 — Humanity's True Origin 48

Chapter 6 — Sin Reframed: Blindness, Not Legal Guilt ... 52

Chapter 7 — Repentance: Awakening, Not Grovelling 58

Chapter 8 — Union: The Reality Beneath Everything 60

Chapter 9 — Identity Before Behaviour 62

SECTION III - THE CROSS WITHOUT VIOLENCE 64

Chapter 10 — Why Jesus Died — And Why We Misunderstood It ... 65

Chapter 11 — Co-Crucifixion and the Death of the False Self 67

Chapter 12 — Forgiveness: God's Eternal Yes 69

Chapter 13 — Salvation Reframed: Healing, Not Escape 71

Chapter 14 — Judgment: Truth Revealed, Not Vengeance Executed 73

Chapter 15 — Hell Without Abandonment...77

Chapter 16 — Resurrection: The Goal, Not the Escape....................85

SECTION IV - THE KINGDOM HERE AND NOW............................87

Chapter 17 — The Kingdom Is the Source 88

Chapter 18 — Prayer as Alignment, Not Persuasion........................90

Chapter 19 — Provision Without Anxiety..95

Chapter 20 — Healing Without Blame 97

Chapter 21 — Authority Without Domination 101

Chapter 22 — Discernment, Conscience, and the Spirit's Voice.....103

Chapter 23 — Spiritual Warfare Reframed: Truth, Not Combat 105

Chapter 24 — Mission Without Threat..106

Chapter 25 — The Church as Family, Not Hierarchy 110

SECTION V - FORMATION WITHOUT FEAR 111

Chapter 26 — Formation Begins With Belonging 112

Chapter 27 — The Body as Participant, Not Obstacle....................114

Chapter 28 — Desire Healed, Not Suppressed 116

Chapter 29 — Transformation Is Slow, Organic, and Real.............117

Chapter 30 — Practices as Alignment, Not Payment 118

Chapter 31 — Failure as Information, Not Disqualification 119

Chapter 32 — Sexuality, Covenant, and Consent 120

Chapter 33 — Trauma, Truth, and Responsibility.......................... 121

Chapter 34 — Boundaries, Authority, and Spiritual Abuse 122

Chapter 35 — Unity Without Coercion... 123

Chapter 36 — Children, Parenting, and Formation......................... 125

Chapter 37 — Lament, Grief, and Protest 128

SECTION VI - WHEN FEAR-BASED FAITH FALLS APART 130

Chapter 38 — When Faith Unravels, It Is Often Maturing 131

Chapter 39 — You Are Not Backsliding — You Are Waking Up...... 134

Chapter 40 — Grieving What You Are Losing 136

Chapter 41 — Jesus Is Not What Is Being Deconstructed 137

Chapter 42 — If Faith Only Worked Through Fear, It Was Never Free 138

Chapter 43 — Jesus Is Often Found in the Wreckage 140

Chapter 44 — Reconstruction Without Panic 143

Chapter 45 — Start With Jesus, Not Answers 146

Chapter 46 — Beware of Replacing One Certainty With Another ... 149

Chapter 47 — Guidance for Pastors, Leaders, and Companions.... 152

Chapter 48 — Losing Christianity Is Not Losing Christ................... 155

Chapter 49 — What to Hold Onto When Everything Feels Uncertain 157

Chapter 50 — When You Fear You Might Be Wrong 161

Chapter 51 — You Are Not Losing Truth — You Are Losing Fear .. 162

SECTION VII - THE STORY WE LIVE INSIDE 163

Chapter 52 — The Story Is Not About Escape — It Is About Healing 164

Chapter 53 — The World Is Not God-Forsaken — It Is God-Haunted 166

Chapter 54 — The Kingdom Is Not a Place — It Is a Way of Being 167

Chapter 55 — What This Gospel Forms in People 169

Chapter 56 — The Church as a Community of the Healed and Healing 171

Chapter 57 — Power, Politics, and the Way of Jesus 173

Chapter 58 — Judgment, Hope, and the Refusal to Abandon Anyone 174

Chapter 59 — Death Is Not the Final Horizon 175

Chapter 60 — Living the Age to Come Now 178

Chapter 61 — The Final Shape of the Gospel 179

FINAL DECLARATION — The Story We Live Inside 180

APPENDIX A — FEAR-BASED VS UNION-BASED CHRISTIANITY 185

APPENDIX B — WHEN THIS THEOLOGY IS MISUNDERSTOOD 188

APPENDIX C — A PASTORAL GUIDE FOR THOSE DECONSTRUCTING 201

APPENDIX D — THE KINGDOM CREED 206

APPENDIX E — THE WITNESS OF THE EARLY CHURCH 207

APPENDIX F — Fear-Based Mission vs Witness-Based Mission ... 218

FINAL WORD TO THE READER 221

PREFACE

How to Read This Book Without Fear

This book was not written to win arguments.
It was written to tell the truth about Jesus — clearly, gently, and without fear.

Many books begin by trying to persuade.
This one begins by trying to make room.

Room to breathe.
Room to be honest.
Room for questions that were never dangerous — only suppressed.
Room for a God who looks like Jesus, not like the fear many of us were taught to call faith.

If you are opening this book cautiously, that makes sense.
Many of us learned to read theology with our shoulders tense and our guard up — as if one wrong thought might cost us belonging, safety, or God Himself.

This book is not written to corner you, correct you, or pressure you into agreement.

It is written to create a safe place to look at Jesus again — without panic.

Who This Book Is For

This book is for:

- Those who love Jesus but no longer know what to do with the fear that surrounded Him.

- Those who were sincere, faithful, and devoted — and still found themselves wounded.

- Those who stayed longer than they should have because leaving felt like failure.

- Those who left quickly because staying felt like a betrayal of conscience.

- Those who were told that certainty was faith — and discovered it wasn't.

- Those who are afraid they might be losing Christianity, when in fact they may finally be finding Christ.

It is also for pastors, leaders, and shepherds who feel the quiet tension between what they were taught to protect and what they now see in Jesus.

If you are confident and settled, this book will not attack you.
If you are weary or unsure, it will not pressure you.
If you are wounded, it will not rush you.

What This Book Is — and What It Is Not

This book is not a manifesto.
It is not a reactionary project.
It is not an attempt to replace one rigid system with another.

It is not anti-Scripture.
It is not anti-holiness.
It is not anti-Church, anti-mission, or anti-truth.
And it is certainly not casual about Jesus.

This book is Jesus-centred — not as a slogan, but as a governing reality. It takes seriously His life, His words, His posture, His refusal to coerce, and His consistent exposure of fear-based religion.

It does not ask, *"Is this familiar?"*
It asks, *"Does this look like Jesus?"*

Where tradition aligns with Him, it is honoured.
Where tradition obscures Him, it is questioned.
Where fear has been used to control, it is named — not to shame the Church, but to protect the people.

Nothing here requires agreement to continue reading.
Nothing demands allegiance.
Nothing is threatened by honest disagreement.

Truth does not need fear to survive.

How to Read This Book

This matters!

This book is not meant to be read like a legal document, a doctrinal checklist, or a debate transcript.
It is not a system to master.
It is a vision to sit with.

Read slowly.
Some chapters may feel familiar.
Others may feel unfamiliar — or unsettling.

Do not rush to resolve tension.
Unresolved questions are not spiritual danger; they are often the beginning of discernment.

Notice fear — but don't obey it.

If anxiety rises, pause.
Fear speaks with urgency.
Love does not.

Ask yourself:

- What exactly feels threatening here?

- Is this challenging God — or a framework I was given about God?

- Does this move me toward love, honesty, and life — or toward control and panic?

Fear is rarely the voice of truth.
It is often the echo of old conditioning.

You are not required to agree.
Agreement is not the goal.
Formation is.

You are free to say:

- "I'm not sure."

- "I need time."

- "I disagree — but I feel more human reading this."

Jesus never demanded instant agreement.
He invited trust — and allowed people to walk.

Let Jesus interpret everything.

If something here feels confronting, return to Him:

- How does Jesus treat people?

- How does He handle doubt?

- How does He respond to fear-based religion?

- Who does He protect?

- Who does He confront?

This book does not ask you to trust its conclusions more than Christ.
It asks you to trust Christ enough to question what does not resemble Him.

Pay attention to fruit.

The test of theology is not how airtight it sounds,
but what it produces.

Does it lead to:

- greater love?

- deeper humility?

- restored agency?

- courage without coercion?

- faith without panic?

Jesus said truth would be known by its fruit — not by how threatening it feels to inherited systems.

A Pastoral Word Before You Begin

If you were taught that questioning is dangerous,
that certainty equals faith,
that fear is a sign of reverence,
that leaving harmful systems is betrayal,
or that God's love is fragile and conditional —

please hear this clearly:

Nothing honest separates you from God.
Nothing sincere puts you at risk.
Nothing true requires fear to defend it.

If something false begins to fall apart as you read,
it is not because you are losing faith —
it is because faith is growing stronger than fear.

You do not need to brace yourself for God.
You do not need to protect Him from your questions.
You do not need to hurry.

Jesus is not found on the other side of panic.
He is found where fear loosens its grip.

Read at the pace of trust.
Stop when you need to.
Return when you're ready.

You are not being tested here.
You are being invited.

And Jesus has always been better than we were ever told.

WHY THIS BOOK EXISTS

Re-Centring Jesus When the Gospel Has Been Framed by Fear

This book exists because something essential has been misplaced.

For many, Christianity no longer sounds like good news.
Not because Jesus has failed —
but because the frameworks built around Him often no longer resemble Him.

Across churches, movements, and traditions, the Gospel has been reshaped into something Jesus never taught:

- fear as motivation

- threat as urgency

- control as discipleship

- belief as compliance

- salvation as escape

What was meant to awaken people into life has too often trained them to manage anxiety, suppress conscience, and endure God rather than trust Him.

This book does not exist to attack Christianity.
It exists because Jesus deserves better than what has been attributed to Him.

The Core Problem This Book Addresses

The central issue is not modern culture, moral decline, politics, or doubt.

The issue is misrepresentation.

When God is portrayed as:

- intermittently loving

- conditionally present

- easily offended

- obsessed with punishment

- divided against Himself

people are forced into impossible positions.

They either submit through fear, pretend through performance, or leave in order to remain honest.

None of those outcomes resemble the fruit of Jesus' life.

This book exists to say something simple and unavoidable:

if Jesus truly reveals God,

then anything that contradicts His character must be re-examined —

even when it is familiar, traditional, or widely defended.

Why Re-Centring Jesus Changes Everything

Jesus does not come to support a system.
He comes to reveal reality.

He does not modify religion —
He exposes where it has drifted from love.

If Jesus is:

- the exact image of God
- the full revelation of divine character
- the lens through which Scripture is understood

then theology cannot begin with fear, law, or threat and later "add grace."

It must begin — and remain — with Him.

Starting anywhere else distorts everything that follows:

- sin becomes legal guilt instead of lost identity
- repentance becomes grovelling instead of awakening
- holiness becomes anxiety instead of shared life
- judgment becomes punishment instead of truth revealed
- mission becomes coercion instead of witness

Re-centring Jesus is not a stylistic preference.
It is a theological necessity.

Why This Matters Now

Many are not leaving Christianity because they want less truth.
They are leaving because they want truth without distortion.

They are not rejecting God.
They are rejecting versions of God that look nothing like Jesus.

This book exists to say:

If something collapses when fear is removed,
it was never built on love.

And if Jesus is as good as the Gospels claim,
then clarity is not dangerous —
it is faithful.

What This Book Is Actually Doing

This is not a deconstruction manual.
It is a re-anchoring.

Not in reaction.
Not in trend.
Not in ideology.

But in the person of Jesus Christ —
and the reality He reveals about God, humanity, salvation, judgment, the Kingdom, and the future of creation.

What follows is an integrated, Jesus-centred vision that draws from:

- Scripture read through Christ

- the early Church's participatory and restorative theology

- pastoral experience with real harm, real faith, and real healing

We begin where all theology must begin:

Not with what we were taught to fear —
but with who Jesus actually is.

INTRODUCTION

Good News Without Fear
Why Jesus Still Sounds Better Than What Many Were Taught

Somewhere along the way, many of us realised something unsettling.

We loved Jesus.
But we were no longer sure we loved the version of faith built around Him.

The disconnect was not sudden.
It was gradual.
Subtle.
Often unnamed.

We listened carefully.
We served faithfully.
We prayed sincerely.

And yet beneath the surface, something did not rest.

The Gospel was called good news, but it often felt like pressure.
God was called love, but often sounded volatile.
Grace was preached, but fear was the atmosphere.
Holiness was honoured, but anxiety was the fuel.

And still — Jesus Himself kept sounding better than what we were told to believe about Him.

This book begins there.

Not with rebellion.
Not with cynicism.
Not with the desire to dismantle faith.

But with a quiet, persistent recognition:

If Jesus truly reveals God, then the Gospel should sound like good news — not like something we must survive.

The Good News (Stated Plainly)

Before anything else is explored — before doctrine, judgment, salvation, or the future — the Good News itself must be named clearly.

The Gospel Jesus proclaimed is not a message about escaping punishment, avoiding hell, or persuading God to be merciful.

The Good News is this:

God is exactly like Jesus.
There is no other God hiding behind Him.

God has never been against humanity.
There was no moment when love withdrew and needed to be convinced to return.

In Jesus Christ, God has united Himself to humanity — permanently and without reserve.
Union is not something we manufacture through belief or behaviour.
It is the reality disclosed in Christ — a reality we awaken to, not one we earn.

The Kingdom of God is not postponed.

It has already arrived — and it continues to press further in, becoming visible wherever life, healing, and love are trusted.

Salvation is not escape from the world.
It is the healing of humanity and the restoration of creation.

Repentance is not grovelling for forgiveness.
It is awakening to reality.

Judgment is not love failing.
It is love telling the truth so that healing can occur.

Death is not the final word.
Resurrection and restoration are.

This is the Gospel Jesus announced:
that God is for us, with us, and committed to making all things new —
and that we are invited to wake up, trust this good news, and live from it without fear.

When the Gospel Stops Sounding Like Good News

For many, the trouble did not begin with disbelief.
It began with exhaustion.

Trying to reconcile:

- a God said to be loving, yet framed as dangerous

- a salvation said to be secure, yet constantly threatened

- a faith said to be freeing, yet governed by fear of getting it wrong

We were told:

- fear was reverence

- certainty was faith

- doubt was danger

- obedience meant silence

- endurance meant holiness

And when something in us resisted — when conscience stirred, when questions emerged, when anxiety spiked — we assumed the problem was us.

But what if it wasn't?

What if the discomfort was not a failure of faith, but a signal that something had been misaligned?

What if the part of you that recoiled from fear-based religion was not drifting from Jesus — but recognising Him?

Jesus Has Always Been the Problem (for Fear-Based Religion)

Jesus was never crucified for being vague, inclusive, or gentle.

He was crucified because He exposed systems that:

- controlled people through fear
- confused God with power
- prioritised certainty over mercy
- protected structures at the expense of people

He healed without permission.
He forgave without leverage.
He welcomed without preconditions.
He told the truth without panic.
And He refused to coerce belief — even when people walked away.

That posture did not disappear after the resurrection.
It was not a temporary teaching strategy.

It was the revelation of God.

So when modern Christianity sounds harsher, more anxious, more punitive, or more controlling than Jesus Himself — the problem is not modern doubt.

It is slow drift — not a sudden rebellion, but a gradual re-centering, where fear, control, and certainty quietly displace the voice and posture of Jesus.

Fear Was Never the Power of the Gospel

Fear can produce compliance.
It cannot produce love.

Fear can modify behaviour temporarily.
It cannot heal desire.

Fear can enforce conformity.
It cannot form Christlikeness.

The early Christian message did not spread because people were terrified of hell.
It spread because people encountered a God who looked like Jesus — and realised they were more loved, more included, and more alive than they had ever imagined.

When fear becomes the primary motivator:

- faith narrows

- conscience weakens

- agency erodes

- honesty becomes dangerous

Many people do not lose faith because they stop caring — they leave because they care too much to pretend.

This book exists for those people.

Before we go further, a brief word about language. Many of the words used throughout this book will be familiar — words you may have heard for years in sermons, prayers, and Scripture readings. But over time, some of these words have absorbed fear, legal assumptions, or meanings Jesus Himself never attached to them. This can make honest reading difficult, not because the words are wrong, but because they have been carrying more weight than they were meant to bear.

The short orientation that follows is not a test of belief or a demand for agreement. It is simply a way of clarifying how certain words and phrases are being used *in this book*, so that you can read without bracing yourself, reacting to unintended meanings, or feeling pressured to keep up. If something feels unfamiliar as you read, let that be an invitation to slow down rather than a signal of danger. Clarity is not the enemy of faith — fear is.

Orientation - How Words Are Used in This Book

A Gentle Orientation for Reading Without Fear

Language shapes perception.

Many of the words and phrases used throughout this book are familiar to Christian readers — words you may have heard for years. But familiarity does not always mean clarity. Over time, some language has absorbed fear, legal assumptions, or meanings Jesus Himself never used.

This short orientation is not here to control interpretation.
It exists to make honest reading possible.

You are not being asked to agree with these definitions before continuing.
You are simply being invited to understand how these words and phrases are being used *in this book* — so that you are not accidentally reacting to meanings that are not intended.

If something feels unfamiliar or unsettling, return here.
Not as a test — but as a reference point.

Agency

What it means here:
Agency is the God-given capacity to perceive, choose, respond, and participate freely in relationship.

It is the ability to say yes or no without coercion, fear, or manipulation.

What it does not mean:
Agency does not mean autonomy from God, self-salvation, or independence from grace.

Why it matters:
Love requires agency. Without real choice, there can be compliance — but not trust, consent, or relationship.

God does not override agency to produce holiness.
He heals it, enlightens it, and invites it.

In short:
Agency is not rebellion.
It is the ground of real love and genuine formation.

Sin

What it means here:
Sin is identity amnesia — living from false beliefs about God, ourselves, and reality.

It is not first a legal problem; it is a relational and perceptual one.

What it does not mean:
Sin is not legal guilt that separates us from God or breaks union.

Why it matters:
Sin damages experience, relationships, and wholeness — but it does not undo Incarnation or union.

In short:
Sin is not who we are.
It is forgetting who we are.

Repentance (Metanoia)

What it means here:
Repentance is awakening — a change of mind, perception, and orientation toward truth.

It is not about emotional remorse for behaviour, but a re-seeing of reality.

What it does not mean:
Repentance is not grovelling, self-hatred, emotional collapse, or earning forgiveness.

Why it matters:
We do not repent to be accepted.
We repent because we already are.

Like the prodigal son, repentance does not restore sonship —
it awakens us to the sonship that never disappeared.

In short:
Belonging precedes repentance.
Love creates the safety that makes honest change possible.

Faith

What it means here:
Faith is relational trust and lived participation in reality as revealed in Jesus.

It is not primarily intellectual certainty — it is relational confidence.

What it does not mean:
Faith is not pressured belief, emotional intensity, or mental agreement used to manage fear.

Why it matters:
Faith grows through trust, presence, and participation — not threat.

In short:
Faith is not thinking something is true.
Faith is living as though it is.

Judgment

What it means here:
Judgment is the revelation of truth.

It is the uncovering of what is real and the exposure of what deforms life.

What it does not mean:
Judgment is not God turning against people or abandoning them to punishment.

Why it matters:
Truth revealed is painful when resisted — but healing when received.

In short:
Judgment is what love does when it refuses to lie.

Wrath

What it means here:
Wrath is love's opposition to everything that destroys life.

It names the collision between love and unreality.

What it does not mean:
Wrath is not divine rage, loss of control, or violence directed at people.

Why it matters:
Love must oppose what deforms and enslaves — or it would not be love.

In short:
Wrath is love refusing to cooperate with destruction.

Holiness

What it means here:
Holiness is participation in God's life.

It is shared life, not separation.

What it does not mean:
Holiness is not fear-based perfectionism or distance from broken people.

Why it matters:
Jesus embodies holiness — and He moves toward brokenness, not away from it.

In short:
Holiness is not distance from brokenness.
It is life present within it.

Salvation

What it means here:
Salvation is healing, restoration, and awakening into union with God.

It addresses being — not merely behaviour.

What it does not mean:
Salvation is not escape from hell or a one-time legal transaction.

Why it matters:
Salvation is not God changing His mind about us.
It is us being healed into reality.

In short:
To be saved is to be made whole.

Hell

What it means here:
Hell is the experience of resisting God's love and truth.

It is real, serious, painful — and restorative in purpose.

What it does not mean:
Hell is not eternal torture, divine vengeance, or separation from God.

Why it matters:
Love does not abandon what it has created, joined, and committed itself to heal.

God's faithfulness outlasts resistance — even when that resistance must be painfully confronted.

In short:
Hell is not the failure of love.
It is love refusing to abandon the soul.

The Kingdom of God

What it means here:
The Kingdom is God's reign and reality made visible.

It is present, active, and embodied.

What it does not mean:
The Kingdom is not a future location, religious system, or political empire.

Why it matters:
Jesus does not ask people to wait for the Kingdom.
He invites them to live from it.

In short:
The Kingdom is not coming someday.
It is breaking in now.

Union

What it means here:
Union is shared life between God and humanity in Christ.

It is an objective reality grounded in the Incarnation.

What it does not mean:
Union is not achieved by belief, effort, or obedience.

Why it matters:
Union does not fluctuate with behaviour.
Awareness of union does.

In short:
We do not move toward union.
We wake up to it.

A Note on Familiar Phrases

Some phrases appear throughout Scripture that have often been interpreted through fear, control, or self-negation. In this book, they are read consistently through Jesus — not through threat-based assumptions.

A brief orientation may help.

"The Fear of God"

How it is often heard:
Being afraid of God — fearing punishment, rejection, or divine anger.

How it is used here:
The fear of God is not terror.
It is awe rooted in trust.

In Scripture, "fear of the Lord" names the moment reality is seen clearly — when illusion collapses and reverence replaces control. It is not anxiety about God's unpredictability; it is recognition of God's goodness, weight, and truth.

Jesus repeatedly says, "Do not be afraid."
He does not remove reverence — He removes terror.

In short:
The fear of God is not being afraid of God.
It is seeing God clearly.

"Take Up Your Cross"

How it is often heard:
Endure suffering, suppress desire, accept abuse, or submit to harm as spiritual obedience.

How it is used here:
To take up the cross is not to seek suffering.
It is to let the false self die.

Jesus is not inviting people into self-erasure, passivity, or harm. He is inviting them to release identities formed in fear, power, and self-protection — and to live from truth, love, and trust instead.

The cross confronts:

- domination

- violence

- ego built on survival

- identities shaped by fear

In short:
Taking up the cross is not about suffering for its own sake.
It is about letting what is false die so life can emerge.

"Deny Yourself"

How it is often heard:
Suppress desire, erase personality, or disappear for the sake of obedience.

How it is used here:
Self-denial is not self-rejection.
It is the refusal to live from a false self.

Jesus does not ask people to deny their humanity.
He asks them to deny the lies that distort it.

To deny oneself is to stop organising life around fear, ego, and survival — and to live from truth instead.

In short:
Self-denial is not becoming less human.
It is becoming truly human.

"Die to Self"

How it is often heard:
Lose identity, suppress needs, or submit to harm as spiritual maturity.

How it is used here:
Dying to self is not annihilation.
It is transformation.

What dies is not the self God created, but the self constructed in fear, shame, and separation. What emerges is not emptiness, but freedom.

In short:
What dies is what is false.
What lives is what is true.

"Count the Cost"

How it is often heard:
Brace for loss, suffering, or punishment as proof of faithfulness.

How it is used here:
Jesus invites people to consider whether they are willing to let go of identities, securities, and power structures that cannot survive love.

The cost is not suffering for suffering's sake.
The cost is releasing control.

In short:
Counting the cost is not preparing for punishment.
It is choosing truth over fear.

A Final Word on Language

These words and phrases were never meant to control people.
They were meant to free them.

If a reading of Scripture produces fear, self-erasure, or justification of harm, it is not being read through Jesus.

This orientation is not a demand for agreement.
It is an invitation to read without panic.

Let Jesus remain the measure.
Let fruit remain the test.
Let love remain the guide.

And take your time.

DOCTRINAL MAP

The Story That Holds Everything Together

This theology is not built from disconnected doctrines.
It is a single, coherent movement — a story that unfolds from God's own life.

What follows is a simple map of that movement.
Not as a system to master,
but as a reality to inhabit.

Incarnation → makes Union inevitable

Union → reframes the Cross

The Cross → leads inexorably to Resurrection

Resurrection → guarantees Restoration

This is not optimism.
It is not denial.

It is the internal logic of a God who is love.

SECTION I - SEEING CLEARLY AGAIN

Jesus, Scripture, and the End of Fear-Based Faith

Chapter 1 — Jesus as the Final Revelation of God

Every theology begins somewhere.
Some begin with doctrine.
Some begin with inherited systems.
Some — quietly — begin with fear.

Jesus begins somewhere else.
He begins with revelation.

When Jesus speaks of God, He does not offer a theory.
He does not construct a system.
He does not point beyond Himself.

He says, *"Anyone who has seen Me has seen the Father."*

This is not poetic exaggeration.
It is a claim of decisive clarity.

Jesus is not one image of God among many.
He is not a corrective voice added to an already complete picture.
He is not a softer version of a harsher deity.

He is the clearest, fullest, and final unveiling of who God is.

This matters more than it first appears.

Because every fear-based theology — no matter how refined — begins by placing something above or beside Jesus:

- a system that must be protected

- a doctrine that must be preserved

- a reading of Scripture that cannot be questioned

- a version of God that Jesus must somehow *balance* rather than reveal

Jesus refuses all of this.

He does not explain God.
He embodies God.

He does not say, *"God is like this."*
He says, *"If you want to know God, look at Me."*

This leads to a decisive conclusion that governs everything that follows:

God has always been like Jesus.
Jesus does not persuade God to become loving — He reveals the love God has always been.
There is no truer picture of God than the life, words, and posture of Christ.

This is not a sentimental claim.
It is a hermeneutical one.

From this point forward, Jesus becomes the measure:

- of Scripture

- of judgment

- of holiness

- of authority

- of salvation

- of power

- of justice

- of what God would never do

If a vision of God contradicts Jesus, Jesus does not need reinterpretation — the vision does.

If a doctrine requires fear where Jesus consistently brings freedom, it is not revealing God accurately — no matter how familiar or well-defended it is.

If an image of God requires coercion, violence, shame, exclusion, or terror to function, it is not revealing God.
It is revealing humanity's fear projected onto God.

Jesus does not soften God.
He unmasks our distortions.

Anything that cannot survive being placed in the presence of Jesus was never true of God to begin with.

Anchor Texts:
John 1:18; John 14:9; Colossians 1:15–20; Hebrews 1:1–3

Chapter 2 — The Doctrine of the Incarnation

God's Irrevocable Union with Humanity

Much Christian theology speaks about Jesus constantly —
yet rarely pauses to say plainly what the Incarnation actually means.

As a result, many doctrines remain unstable:

- union is proclaimed but left floating

- salvation is preached but detached from embodiment

- restoration is hoped for but not grounded

- fear-based systems survive because nothing has finally changed at the level of being

The Incarnation resolves this.

The Incarnation is not merely the method by which salvation happens.
It is the event that permanently changes reality.

In Jesus Christ, God does not visit humanity.
God unites Himself to humanity — **forever**.

What the Incarnation Is

The Incarnation is the eternal Son of God taking on real, full, unceasing humanity.

Not as a disguise, experiment, or temporary strategy — but as an irrevocable union.

In Jesus:

- God becomes human without ceasing to be God

- humanity is taken into God without being erased

- divinity and humanity are united without confusion, domination, or separation

This union is **ontological**, not symbolic.

Jesus does not save us *from* humanity.
He saves us *as* humanity.

Jesus Is Not Merely Like Us — He Is Us

Jesus does not stand over humanity as an exception.
He stands within humanity as its fulfilment.

He assumes human nature — not just an individual body.
What happens to Him happens *within humanity itself*.

His life, death, resurrection, and ascension are not private events.
They are **human events**.

This is why the early Church spoke of Christ as:

- the Second Adam

- the New Humanity

- the recapitulation of all things

Jesus does not replace humanity.
He redefines it from the inside.

The Incarnation Is God's "Yes" to Humanity — Permanently

In Jesus, God does not merely forgive humanity.
He binds Himself to humanity.

The ascension is not Jesus leaving humanity behind.
It is humanity taken into God.

This means:

- God does not revert to distance

- God does not relate externally ever again

- humanity is now carried within the life of God

Separation theology collapses here.

Union Is Not a Reward — It Is a Reality

Because of the Incarnation:

union is not achieved
union is not conditional
union is not fragile

Faith does not create union.
Repentance does not manufacture it.
They awaken us to what the Incarnation has already secured.

Obedience does not earn union.
It flows from the discovery of what is already true.

Salvation is not God crossing a distance.
It is humanity waking up to closeness.

The Incarnation Secures Bodies, Creation, and Matter

Because God became flesh:

- bodies matter eternally

- creation is not disposable

- matter is not inferior

- resurrection is essential

Any theology that treats salvation as escape from materiality is not Incarnational Christianity.

God does not despise the flesh He comes to heal.

The Incarnation guarantees:

- bodily resurrection

- new creation

- healed desire

- redeemed time, space, and matter

The Incarnation in One Sentence

"The Incarnation means that God has joined Himself to humanity in Jesus Christ, permanently and without reserve, making union the unchangeable reality of human existence and the foundation of all salvation, judgment, healing, and restoration."

Christianity does not *centre* sin as its starting point.
It centres the Incarnation — God's irrevocable union with humanity — and understands sin in the light of that union, not the other way around.

Everything else flows from there.

Anchor Texts:
John 1:14; Hebrews 2:14–17; Colossians 2:9; Ephesians 1:9–10

Chapter 3 — How Scripture Is Meant to Be Read

Many people who arrive at fear-based faith did not lose trust in God first.

They lost trust in how Scripture was used.

They were told the Bible was clear — until it wasn't.
They were told it was harmonious — until it contradicted itself.
They were told it revealed God — until God began to look nothing like Jesus.

The problem was never Scripture itself.
The problem was the expectation placed upon it.

Scripture is not a single-voiced document.
It is a library.

It contains:

- poetry and protest

- law and lament

- wisdom and warfare

- revelation and misunderstanding

- growth, correction, and development

It records humanity's real encounter with God across time — not dictation flattened into a rulebook.

Scripture is always spoken **from somewhere**.
It is written at particular moments, to particular people, facing particular pressures.
Kings, prophets, poets, priests, apostles — all speak from within their historical, cultural, and moral horizons.

This does not weaken Scripture.
It tells the truth about how God chooses to speak — not by bypassing humanity, but by working within it.

Ignoring context does not honour Scripture.
It distorts it.
Reading Scripture faithfully requires asking not only *what was said*, but *why it was said*, *to whom*, and *toward what end*.

Jesus knew this.

That is why He did not treat Scripture as static authority to be preserved at all costs.
He treated it as **witness**.

"You search the Scriptures because you think that in them you have life; and it is they that testify about Me."

Scripture does not exist to terminate conversation.
It exists to lead us to Jesus.

And once Jesus is seen clearly, Scripture must be reread.

Jesus quotes Scripture to expose misuse — not to reinforce control.
He reinterprets:

- Sabbath

- law

- purity

- holiness
- sacrifice
- election
- judgment

Often directly contradicting dominant readings of His time.

This tells us something essential:

**Faithfulness to Scripture is not flat repetition.
It is Christ-shaped interpretation.**

There is therefore an order of interpretive authority within Scripture itself — not imposed from outside it:

1. Jesus Himself

2. The Spirit of Christ bearing witness

3. The apostolic witness to Jesus

4. Contextual pastoral writings (letters and teachings addressing specific communities, situations, and stages of formation)

5. The Old Testament moving toward Christ

When tension appears, the higher revelation governs the lower.

Jesus interprets Scripture.
Scripture does not domesticate Jesus.

This is not Scripture diminished.

It is Scripture fulfilled.

The question is no longer, *"Is this verse in the Bible?"*
The question is, *"Does this interpretation look like Jesus?"*

If it does not:

- restore dignity

- increase love

- free conscience

- heal rather than harm

then it must be re-examined.

This is not liberalism.
It is fidelity.

Jesus is not one voice among many.
He is the Word by whom all words are judged.

Anchor Texts:
Luke 24:27; Luke 24:44–45; John 5:39–40; Matthew 22:37-40

Chapter 4 — God Revealed: Love Without Fear

Fear has been one of religion's most effective tools.

Fear motivates compliance.
Fear creates urgency.
Fear produces measurable outcomes.

Fear also distorts everything it touches.

When fear governs theology, God becomes:

- unpredictable

- easily offended

- quick to punish

- obsessed with correctness

- dangerous to approach

Jesus never behaves this way.

Jesus does not use fear as the engine of transformation.

When He encounters the woman caught in adultery, He dismantles the violent system around her before addressing her life.

When He touches the leper, He does not recoil to preserve holiness — He reveals holiness by moving closer.

He does not threaten people into transformation.
He does not shame people into holiness.
He does not coerce belief.

He reveals a God who is:

- consistently good

- relentlessly patient

- uncompromising toward harm

- endlessly restorative

- incapable of abandoning creation

This does not make God permissive.
It makes God faithful.

Fear-based religion claims fear is necessary for reverence.
Jesus exposes the opposite.

Fear does not produce reverence.
Fear produces survival.

Reverence is awe rooted in trust.

The fear of God is not being afraid of God.
It is seeing God clearly.

Perfect love drives out fear — not because fear is sinful, but because fear is unnecessary once love is known.

This is why Jesus repeatedly says, *"Do not be afraid."*

Fear is never presented as spiritual maturity.
It is presented as what love heals.

God's love does not fluctuate with performance.
God's presence does not withdraw in disappointment.
God does not relate through threat.

Judgment, discipline, correction, and transformation all occur —
but they occur **inside love**, never outside it.

Fear-based faith says:
"God will love you if…"

Jesus reveals:
"God loves you. Now come home."

Until God is seen without fear, nothing else can be trusted.

Anchor Texts:
1 John 4:16–18; Matthew 11:28–30; John 3:17; Luke 15

SECTION II - WHAT WENT WRONG — AND WHAT WAS NEVER LOST

Humanity, Sin, and the Lie of Separation

Chapter 5 — Humanity's True Origin

Most Christian frameworks begin the human story with failure.

Genesis 3 becomes the lens through which everything else is read. Humanity is framed as fundamentally broken — separated, guilty, dangerous to God, and in need of fixing.

Jesus never begins there.

Jesus consistently speaks and acts as though humanity has a deeper origin — one not erased by failure, sin, or fear.

Before humanity ever falls, humanity already *is*.

Before sin, humanity is:

- created in God's image

- named "very good"

- given vocation, not probation

- entrusted with participation, not survival

This matters because where you believe humanity begins determines how you believe humanity must be healed.

If humanity begins in failure, salvation must be coercive — a rescue *from* who we are.
If humanity begins in goodness, salvation must be restorative — a return *to* who we have always been.

Jesus clearly believes the latter.

Jesus' Starting Point

Jesus does not approach people as enemies of God.
He does not treat them as worthless sinners who must be convinced to be loved.
He does not shame them into repentance or threaten them into belonging.

Instead, He treats people as:

- lost children

- wounded image-bearers

- enslaved by lies

- confused about who they truly are

He behaves as though they already belong — even when they do not yet know it.

This is why Jesus does not take people back to Adam.
He takes them back to the Father.

The prodigal son is not a story about legal guilt.
It is a story about forgotten sonship.

The sheep is not sought because it is bad.
It is sought because it belongs.

Jesus' ministry only makes sense if humanity's origin is not sin, but God.

Before the Fall — and Before Creation

The New Testament goes even further.

It speaks of humanity as known, intended, and held in Christ before the foundation of the world.

This does not mean humans existed as independent beings before creation.
It means something deeper:

Humanity was always included in God's eternal intention —
always seen through Christ,
always destined for union,
always wanted.

Grace is not a reaction to sin.
Love is not triggered by repentance.
Union is not Plan B.

Jesus does not invent belonging.
 He reveals it.

Restoration, Not Replacement

Jesus does not come to discard humanity.
He comes to restore it.

He does not fix a failed species.
He heals a wounded one.

Humanity's story does not begin with sin.
It begins with God.

And it does not end with escape.
It ends with union revealed, restored, and fully lived.

Sin is not our origin.
Union is.

Anchor Texts:
Genesis 1:26–31; Luke 15; Ephesians 1:3–5; Colossians 1:16–17

Chapter 6 — Sin Reframed: Blindness, Not Legal Guilt

Few words have caused more confusion, fear, and spiritual damage than the word *sin*.

In fear-based theology, sin is commonly framed as:

- legal guilt

- moral stain

- offense demanding punishment

- the reason God withdraws

Within that framework, sin is treated like a crime on a ledger — something that must be paid for, managed, or punished in order to restore divine favour.

Jesus does not use the word this way.

When Jesus speaks of sin, He does not speak like a prosecutor. He speaks like a physician.

He frames sin as:

- blindness

- sickness

- slavery

- lostness

- misalignment

"This is the sin," He says — "that they do not believe."
Not *that they behaved badly*, but that they could not see.

In Jesus' framework, sin is not first about breaking rules.
It is about misperceiving reality — not knowing who God is, and therefore not knowing who you are.

The primary New Testament word translated as *sin*, *hamartia*, literally means *to miss the mark*.
But the mark is not moral perfection.
The mark is true identity — life lived in alignment with reality as revealed in Christ.

Sin is not humanity at its core.
It is humanity disoriented.

Sin Does Not Break Union — It Obscures It

Sin does not rupture God's relationship with humanity.
It contradicts it.

It damages experience, distorts desire, fractures relationships, and diminishes wholeness — but it does not undo the Incarnation or dissolve union.

This distinction changes everything.

Sin hurts — not because God punishes it — but because it violates reality.
When you live against truth, truth pushes back.

Not in anger.
In consequence.

Jesus does not shame sinners.
He heals them.

He does not distance Himself from sin.
He enters it to remove its power.

He does not threaten people out of sin.
He reveals a truer life that makes sin unnecessary.

Sin is not who we are.
It is forgetting who we are.

What About Romans 5? Adam, Death, and the Question of Guilt

Romans 5 is often used to reintroduce fear — especially the idea that guilt is inherited, condemnation is automatic, and humanity begins its story already legally damned.

That is not what Paul says.

Paul does **not** say guilt is inherited.
He says **death spread**.

"Through one man sin entered the world, and death through sin, and so death spread to all."

Death is the condition that spreads — mortality, corruption, fear, and disorientation.
Sin multiplies *within* that condition, but it is not legally transmitted as personal guilt.

Paul's concern in Romans 5 is not courtroom guilt.
It is **enslavement to death**.

Adam introduces a condition humanity did not choose: mortality and alienation.
Christ introduces a condition humanity did not earn: life and restoration.

And Paul is explicit about which is stronger.

If Adam's failure could shape humanity without their consent,
how much more can Christ's faithfulness heal it.

Paul does not say Adam's act condemns individuals by default.
He says Adam's act exposes humanity to death — and within death, sin reigns.

But then Paul turns the entire argument on its head.

Where sin increased, **grace increased all the more**.
Not equally.
Not cautiously.
All the more.

Adam's impact is not the final word.
Christ's life is.

Romans 5 is not about inherited guilt.
It is about **two humanities** — one organised around death, the other around life.

And the point of the passage is not how deeply humanity fell,
but how decisively Christ outpaced the fall.

Death is the enemy.
Death is what reigns.
Death is what Christ confronts.

And death is what Christ defeats.

This is why Paul later says that **the last enemy to be destroyed is death** — not humanity.

Romans 5 does not teach that babies are born condemned.
It teaches that humanity is born into a wounded condition — one Christ has already entered, healed, and overcome.

Sin is not transmitted as guilt.
It is learned as misalignment inside a broken world.

Grace, by contrast, is not reactive.
It is original.

Sin as Tragedy, Not Condemnation

This is why Jesus never treats sin as a reason to withdraw.

He treats it as a reason to draw near.

He does not say, "You are guilty — therefore God is distant."
He says, "You are lost — therefore you are sought."

He does not approach sinners as enemies of God.
He approaches them as people living beneath their true identity.

Sin is serious — but not because it angers God.
It is serious because it dehumanises people.

Fear-based theology treats sin as rebellion to crush.
Jesus treats sin as deception to expose and heal.

That is why repentance is awakening, not grovelling.
That is why forgiveness precedes confession.
That is why belonging comes before behaviour.

Sin is not the end of the story.
It was never meant to be.

Christ did not come to manage guilt.
He came to heal humanity.

And where sin once reigned in death,
life now reigns through grace.

Sin is not who we are.
It is forgetting who we are.

Anchor Texts:
John 16:9; Romans 5:12–21; Luke 19:10; 2 Corinthians 4:4; Mark 7:21–23

Chapter 7 — Repentance: Awakening, Not Grovelling

If sin has been misunderstood, repentance has been nearly unrecognisable.

Repentance has been taught as:

- grovelling

- self-hatred

- emotional collapse

- repeated apology

- moral probation

The word Jesus uses — *metanoia* — means none of these things.

It literally means a change of mind or perception — It is not about emotional remorse for behaviour, but a re-seeing of reality.

In lived terms, this awakening looks like:

- a change of mind

- a shift in perception

- an awakening to reality

Repentance is not turning toward God from distance.
It is waking up to the God who was already present.

The clearest picture Jesus gives of repentance is the prodigal son.

The son does not repent by rehearsing shame.
He repents when he *comes to his senses*.

The Father does not wait for repentance to forgive.
He runs before the speech is finished.

Repentance does not make God willing.
It makes us receptive.

We do not repent to be accepted.
We repent because we already are.

The prodigal does not return to *become* a son.
He returns because he *never stopped being a son*.

Repentance is not what secures belonging.
Belonging is what makes repentance possible.

This is why true repentance produces freedom, not fear.

It does not crush identity.
It restores it.

Anchor Texts:
Mark 1:15; Luke 15:17–24; Romans 2:4; 2 Corinthians 7:10

Chapter 8 — Union: The Reality Beneath Everything

Union is not the reward of salvation.
Union is the foundation of salvation.

This is where many theologies quietly fracture.

They speak of union as something achieved:

- through belief

- through repentance

- through obedience

- through correct doctrine

Jesus speaks of union as something revealed.

"In that day you will realise that I am in the Father,
and you are in Me,
and I am in you."

Union does not fluctuate with behaviour.
Awareness of union does.

Paul does not say we are *becoming* one spirit with the Lord.
He says we *are*.

This is not mystical exaggeration.
It is Paul's settled theological claim about what has already occurred in Christ.

Union is not fragile.
It is not reversible.
It is not earned.

It is the consequence of Incarnation.

When God joins Himself to humanity in Christ, separation becomes a lie — even if it still feels real.

Salvation is not God crossing a distance.
It is humanity waking up to closeness.

Union does not erase responsibility.
It makes responsibility meaningful.

You cannot be separated from God —
but you can live as though you are.

And that belief shapes everything.

Anchor Texts:
John 14:20; 1 Corinthians 6:17; Colossians 3:3; Romans 8:38–39

Chapter 9 — Identity Before Behaviour

The Jesus-story never begins formation with behaviour.

Before ministry, obedience, or sacrifice, identity is named.

At Jesus' baptism, the Father declares:

"This is my beloved Son."

This declaration comes before ministry, obedience, or sacrifice.

Fear-based religion reverses the order:

behave correctly → become accepted

prove worth → receive belonging

Jesus restores the original order:

belonging → transformation

identity → alignment

Righteousness is not a legal status covering a sinful core.
It is a new nature revealed in Christ.

"As He is, so are we in this world."

This does not deny struggle.
It redefines it.

Sin is no longer evidence of worthlessness.
It is evidence of misalignment.

Growth is no longer earning.
It is remembering.

Holiness is no longer distance from brokenness.
It is the presence of life within it.

When identity stabilises, behaviour follows.

Fear restrains behaviour temporarily.
Love reshapes desire permanently.

Jesus trusts identity more than threat.

And He is right.

Anchor Texts:
Matthew 3:16–17; 1 John 4:17; Romans 8:15–17; Galatians 4:6–7

SECTION III - THE CROSS WITHOUT VIOLENCE

Salvation, Forgiveness, Judgment, Hell, and Resurrection

Chapter 10 — Why Jesus Died — And Why We Misunderstood It

The cross sits at the centre of Christian faith —
and yet it is one of the most misunderstood events in history.

Many were taught that Jesus died to change God's attitude toward humanity.
That the cross was the moment when love finally overcame wrath.
That violence was required for forgiveness.
That God needed blood in order to be merciful.

Jesus never frames His death this way.

The cross does not reveal a God who needed to be persuaded to forgive.
It reveals a God who was willing to be misunderstood, rejected, and killed rather than stop loving.

Jesus does not die to rescue us from the Father.
He dies to rescue us from lies about God — and from the powers of fear, sin, and death those lies sustain.

The Question the Cross Actually Answers

The cross does not answer, *"How can God forgive?"*
Jesus forgives freely before the cross.

The cross answers a deeper question:

What happens when divine love collides with human fear, power, and violence?

The answer is not retaliation.
It is self-giving love that absorbs violence without reproducing it.

Jesus does not expose God's wrath.
He exposes ours.

The cross reveals what humanity does to God when God refuses to dominate.

Atonement Without Divine Violence

The New Testament uses many images to speak about the cross — but none require reading the Father as violently punishing the Son in order to become merciful.
The cross reveals God's self-giving love, not a division within God.

It says:

- God was in Christ, reconciling the world to Himself

- Jesus entered our death to destroy death from within

- He bore sin — not punishment

- He absorbed hostility and returned forgiveness

The cross is not a transaction inside God.
It is a revelation of God.

God does not require sacrifice to love.
God *becomes* the sacrifice to heal.

The cross is not about satisfying divine justice.
It is about unveiling divine faithfulness.

Anchor Texts:
Luke 23:34; 2 Corinthians 5:19; Colossians 2:14–15; Hebrews 2:14

Chapter 11 — Co-Crucifixion and the Death of the False Self

The cross is not only something Jesus does *for* us.
It is something that happens *to* us.

Paul does not say, "Jesus was crucified so you don't have to change."
He says, "I have been crucified with Christ."

This is not metaphorical poetry.
Paul presents co-crucifixion as ontological participation, not inspirational language.
It is participatory reality.

What Dies on the Cross

What dies is not your humanity.
What dies is the false self — the self constructed in fear, separation, shame, and survival.

The cross confronts:

- the lie that you are alone

- the lie that you must earn love

- the lie that power comes from domination

- the lie that God is against you

Jesus takes these lies into death —
not to punish them,
but to end their authority.

This is why the cross feels threatening to systems built on fear.

The cross dismantles every structure that depends on:

- exclusion

- scapegoating

- punishment

- control

Participation, Not Substitution

Jesus does not stand in our place so that nothing changes.
He stands *with* us so that everything can change.

We are not spectators at the cross.
We are included.

The old self dies —

not because God demands it,

but because a false self cannot survive the presence of love.

Anchor Texts:
Galatians 2:20; Romans 6:6–8; Colossians 3:1–3

Chapter 12 — Forgiveness: God's Eternal Yes

Forgiveness is not a decision God makes after the cross.
It is who God has always been.

Jesus forgives sins freely — publicly — scandalously — before the cross.
This does not minimise the cross; it reveals what the cross unveils.

He forgives:

- without sacrifice

- without confession formulas

- without leverage

The cross does not begin God's forgiveness.
It reveals the depth of a forgiveness that was already flowing — even while it was being rejected.

Forgiveness Is Not Pretending Harm Didn't Happen

Forgiveness does not deny justice.
It transcends retaliation.

It does not erase accountability.
It removes vengeance.

Forgiveness is not God lowering His standards.
It is God refusing to let violence define reality.

On the cross, Jesus prays:

"Father, forgive them — they do not know what they are doing."

This is not weakness.
It is clarity.

Forgiveness flows from seeing truth.

God forgives because God sees fully.

Anchor Texts:
Mark 2:5–12; Luke 7:47–50; Ephesians 1:7; Acts 3:19

Chapter 13 — Salvation Reframed: Healing, Not Escape

Salvation has often been framed as rescue from punishment.
Jesus frames it as restoration to life.

Salvation is not primarily about the afterlife.
It is about *this life healed*.

Jesus saves people from:

- blindness

- bondage

- shame

- exclusion

- false identity

He does not save them *from God*.
He saves them *into God*.

Salvation is not a legal status applied externally.
It is life restored internally.

To be saved is to be made whole.

Salvation Is Participatory

Salvation is not something God does *instead of* us.
It is something God does *with* us and *within* us.

We are saved as we awaken to union.

This does not minimise sin.
It renders sin unnecessary.

Not by denying consequence, but by restoring desire and identity.

Anchor Texts:
Luke 19:9–10; John 10:10; Titus 3:5; James 5:19–20

Chapter 14 — Judgment: Truth Revealed, Not Vengeance Executed

Judgment has often been framed as divine anger finally unleashed — as the moment when patience runs out and punishment begins.

Jesus reveals judgment very differently.

Judgment is not love failing.
It is love telling the truth.

When light enters darkness, darkness is exposed — not punished.
Exposure is not violence.
It is clarity.

Jesus says judgment happens when light is revealed and people respond to it.
Some receive it.
Some resist it.
But the light itself does not change.

This is not courtroom language.
It is diagnostic language.

The New Testament word *krisis* — translated as *judgment* — refers to discernment, separation, and exposure.
It names the moment reality becomes unavoidable.

Judgment, in Jesus' teaching, is what happens when truth is no longer hidden —
when lies lose cover,
when illusion collapses,
when what is real stands revealed.

Wrath Without Rage

Much confusion around judgment comes from misunderstanding *wrath*.

In Scripture, wrath is not divine volatility, emotional rage, or loss of control.
It is not God "snapping."

Wrath names God's settled, unwavering opposition to everything that destroys life.

It is not directed *at* people.
It is directed *toward* what enslaves, deforms, and dehumanises them.

Wrath is not a mood God enters.
It is love refusing to cooperate with death, lies, and violence.

Because God is love, He must oppose what destroys love's creatures.
Anything less would not be mercy — it would be indifference.

This is why wrath in Scripture is consistently linked with patience, endurance, and restraint —
not impulsive retaliation.

Wrath is not love losing control.
It is love refusing to abandon the truth.

Justice Is Not Retribution

Judgment is often confused with justice —
and justice is often confused with punishment.

But biblical justice is not retribution.
It is restoration.

Retributive systems ask:
Who deserves what?

Jesus asks:
What has gone wrong — and how is it healed?

Justice in the Kingdom is not about balancing pain with pain.
It is about setting things right.

This does not remove accountability.
It deepens it.

Truth is revealed.
Harm is named.
Responsibility is faced.
Repair becomes possible.

But vengeance is never the goal.

God does not judge in order to "get even."
God judges in order to make things whole.

Judgment Is Always Redemptive in God

God's judgments in Scripture are never arbitrary.
They are always aimed at:

- liberation

- repentance

- restoration

Even when judgment is severe, it is never abandonment.

God does not judge to destroy.
God judges to heal what lies have broken.

Judgment exposes what is false so that what is true can live.
It confronts illusion so that freedom becomes possible.

Judgment, therefore, is not the opposite of mercy.
It is mercy refusing to lie.

Truth revealed can be painful —
but truth resisted is what keeps people bound.

Judgment reveals reality.
And reality, in the hands of love, always serves life.

Anchor Texts:
John 3:19–21; John 12:47–48; Luke 12:2–3; Hebrews 4:12–13

Chapter 15 — Hell Without Abandonment

Fire, Judgment, and the Refusal of Love to Let Go

Few ideas in Christianity have produced more fear, confusion, and spiritual harm than the idea of hell.

For many, hell was taught as the ultimate threat — the place God sends those who fail to believe correctly, behave sufficiently, or repent convincingly. It was framed as eternal separation, divine rejection, and endless punishment. For some, it became the silent backdrop of faith: shaping prayer through anxiety, motivating obedience through fear, and training people to manage God rather than trust Him.

That version of hell did not come from Jesus.

When hell is read through Jesus — not through later tradition, fear-based control systems, or medieval imagination — it emerges not as God's final word over humanity, but as a serious, painful, and confrontational encounter with truth.
It is not abandonment.
It is not vengeance.
And it is not love failing.
It is love refusing to lie.

What Jesus Actually Said — and What He Didn't

Jesus does not use the modern concept of "hell" as it is often preached.

In the Gospels, His primary warning language is **Gehenna** — a real valley outside Jerusalem, historically associated with burning refuse, prophetic judgment, and national catastrophe. Gehenna was not metaphysical geography. It was symbolic, embodied language used to speak urgently about trajectories that destroy life, community, and identity here and now.

Jesus uses this language precisely because these trajectories can harden beyond the present life — truth does not stop being true at death.

Jesus' warnings about Gehenna are not threats of God's rejection.
They are interventions.

They are spoken to living people about paths that are already producing death — inwardly and relationally. Jesus warns because He loves. He exposes because He heals. He interrupts destruction before it hardens into permanence.

Jesus does not threaten people with abandonment.
He confronts what is killing them.

Gehenna, Hades, and the Lake of Fire — Naming the Distinctions

Much confusion about hell comes from collapsing distinct biblical images into one fear-based concept. Scripture does not do this.

Gehenna

Gehenna is Jesus' primary warning language.
It names the lived experience of destruction that comes from resisting truth, clinging to violence, domination, hypocrisy, or self-protective religion. It is this-worldly, relational, and embodied, even when it gestures beyond the present.

Gehenna is not God sending people away.
It is God urgently calling people back.

Hades / Sheol

Hades (Greek) or Sheol (Hebrew) refers to the realm of the dead — the grave, the state of death, the shadowy condition humanity experiences under mortality. Scripture is clear: God is present even there.

"If I make my bed in Sheol, You are there."

Hades is not separation from God.
It is the condition from which God rescues.

The Lake of Fire

The Lake of Fire appears in apocalyptic imagery, especially Revelation. It is not a torture chamber. It is the symbolic fire of God's consuming, purifying presence.

Crucially, Scripture says:
Death and Hades are thrown into the Lake of Fire.

If death itself is destroyed in fire, then fire cannot exist to preserve suffering forever.
Fire is not God's enemy.
Fire is God's love confronting what cannot survive love.

Hell as the Experience of Resisting Love

Hell, as revealed through Jesus, is not a place God sends people.
It is the experience of resisting the truth and love of God.

When love meets resistance, the encounter is painful — not because love has changed, but because illusion is being exposed.

Hell is:

- the pain of clinging to lies

- the suffering of refusing love

- the collapse of false identity

- the burning away of illusion

- the confrontation with truth

It is not God against humanity.
It is humanity resisting reality.

The same presence that feels like heaven to the healed
feels like fire to the resistant.

Not because God shifts posture —
but because the heart has not yet opened.

This is not sentimental language.
It is spiritually and psychologically precise.

Love is not neutral.
Truth is not passive.
Union exposes whatever contradicts it.

Judgment as Fire — Healing, Not Vengeance

Jesus' judgment is never retributive.
It is revelatory.

Judgment, in Jesus' teaching, is what love does when it refuses to collude with lies. It exposes what is false so that what is true can finally live.

Fire in Scripture is not torture.
It is refinement.

Gold is not punished by fire.
It is revealed.

Pruning is not destruction.
It is preparation for fruit.

Light does not punish darkness.
It dispels it.

Hell, therefore, is not love failing.
It is love burning away everything that is not love.

This is why fear-based theology misunderstands judgment. It imagines fire as sadism rather than surgery, vengeance rather than medicine, exclusion rather than purification.

But the fire of God does not exist to preserve evil forever.
It exists to end it.

God Is Not Using Fire — God Is the Fire

Scripture does not say God *wields* fire.
It says God **is** a consuming fire.

This is not a metaphor for anger. It is a revelation of love's intensity. God does not step back and punish from a distance — He draws near, and whatever cannot survive love is undone by His presence.

Fire is not something God turns on and off.
It is what God is when love confronts what resists it.

To those aligned with truth, this fire heals, warms, and illuminates.
To those clinging to illusion, the same fire burns — not because love has changed, but because resistance has not yet yielded.

Judgment is not God becoming dangerous.
Judgment is love becoming unavoidable.

Hell Is Not Separation From God

Jesus does not portray God's final posture toward humanity as abandonment..

Scripture consistently affirms:

- God's presence is inescapable
- God's love is unwavering
- nothing can separate humanity from God in Christ

Hell is not the absence of God.
It is the presence of God experienced through resistance.

To the open heart, God's presence heals.
To the closed heart, the same presence burns.

Same God.
Same love.
Different posture of reception.

This is why hell cannot be understood as exile from God.
There is no place where God is not.

What burns is not the person.
What burns is the lie.

Hell Is Not the End of the Story

Hell is never presented as God's final word.

Jesus speaks consistently of:

- restoration
- drawing all people to Himself

- the defeat of death

- resurrection, not perpetual ruin

Scripture does not end with souls escaping creation.
It ends with creation healed.

If death is the final enemy — and Scripture says it is — then humanity is not. God destroys death, not people.

Hell exists for a purpose — and that purpose is not punishment.
It is:

- purification

- awakening

- correction

- healing

- the collapse of false identity

Hell does not protect heaven from sinners.
It protects sinners from being permanently lost to lies.

The Final Word Is Not Fire — It Is Love

Jesus is the Alpha and the Omega.
Hell is not.

The final word of Scripture is not threat.
It is renewal.

"Behold, I am making all things new."
Not some things.

Not only the obedient.
All things.

Some Christians refer to this hope as **universal restoration** — the conviction that God's redemptive purposes ultimately outlast resistance and that love, not fear, has the final word.

Hell is the surgeon's knife — not the morgue.
The refiner's fire — not the incinerator.
The mercy of truth — not the triumph of fear.

And even where resistance remains, love does not withdraw.
It waits.
It works.
It burns.
It heals.

Hell is not the end of the story.
Love is.

And if judgment reveals truth,
and love refuses abandonment,
then resurrection is not optional —
it is inevitable.

Anchor Texts

Matthew 25:46; Luke 12:49; 1 Corinthians 3:12–15; Psalm 139:8; Revelation 20–21

Chapter 16 — Resurrection: The Goal, Not the Escape

If judgment reveals truth and hell does not have the final word, then resurrection must.

Resurrection is not an appendix to the Gospel.
It is the Gospel's fulfilment.

Jesus does not rise as a ghost.
Resurrection is God's public commitment to matter, bodies, and creation.
He rises bodily.

Resurrection declares:

- death does not win

- matter matters

- creation is not disposable

- love is stronger than the grave

The resurrection is not Jesus escaping the world.
It is the world being reclaimed.

Resurrection Guarantees Restoration

If Jesus is raised bodily, then:

- humanity is not discarded

- creation is not abandoned

- the future is physical, healed, and whole

Resurrection makes restoration inevitable.

Christian hope is not leaving earth.
It is earth made new.

Anchor Texts:
Luke 24:39; Romans 8:18–23; 1 Corinthians 15; Revelation 21:1–5

SECTION IV - THE KINGDOM HERE AND NOW

Life, Prayer, Provision, Authority, Discernment, and Mission Without Transaction

Chapter 17 — The Kingdom Is the Source

Jesus does not speak of the Kingdom as a distant destination.
He speaks of it as a present reality — already among you, already at hand.

The Kingdom is not something you build in order to receive blessing.
It is the source from which life itself flows.

This reverses religious logic.

Fear-based faith assumes scarcity.
God is reluctant.
Provision is conditional.
Blessing must be earned.

Jesus assumes abundance.
The Father already knows what you need.
The Kingdom is already given.
Life flows from trust, not striving.

When Jesus says, "Seek first the Kingdom of God, and all these things will be added," He is not calling people into anxious spiritual effort.
He is inviting them to re-locate their source.

He does not say *work for* the Kingdom.
He says *live from* it.

When the Kingdom is understood as the source, motivation changes.

Obedience flows from trust, not threat.
Generosity flows from abundance, not anxiety.
Rest becomes possible without guilt.
Work becomes participation, not self-justification.

We do not behave well in order to gain the Kingdom.
We discover the Kingdom — and find our behaviour quietly reshaped from the inside out.

The Kingdom is not fragile.
It does not expand through pressure, fear, or performance.
It becomes visible wherever love is trusted and received.

Jesus shows this again and again — eating with those who had no religious credibility, forgiving without leverage, healing without preconditions.
He does not manufacture the Kingdom through effort.
He reveals it by living from the Father.

And when people encounter that life — unhurried, unafraid, deeply rooted — they do not feel coerced.
They feel invited.

Anchor Texts:
Luke 17:20–21; Matthew 6:33; Romans 14:17

Chapter 18 — Prayer as Alignment, Not Persuasion

Many people learned prayer inside a framework of distance.

God was imagined as "up there."
Humanity was imagined as "down here."
Prayer became the bridge between the two — an attempt to get heaven to move, intervene, or return.

In that framework, prayer was often urgent.
Pleading made sense.
Persistence felt necessary.
Silence felt dangerous.

But Jesus does not pray like someone trying to get God's attention.

He prays from inside relationship.
From shared life.
From union rather than separation.

"Father, I thank You that You have heard Me," He says — before the outcome is visible.

Prayer, as Jesus models it, is not persuasion.
It is alignment.

Prayer Begins Where Union Is Real

If God is distant, prayer becomes effort.
If God is reluctant, prayer becomes pressure.
If God comes and goes, prayer becomes anxiety.

But if union is real, prayer changes its posture entirely.

In Christ, God has not temporarily visited the world — He has joined it.
The Spirit has not been loaned — He has been given.
The Kingdom has not been postponed — it has been inaugurated.

Prayer, therefore, is not about closing a gap between heaven and earth.
It is learning to live awake to a reality already present.

This is why Jesus teaches His disciples to pray,
"Your Kingdom come,"
not as a demand for arrival,
but as an invitation for visibility.

Prayer does not make God willing.
It makes us receptive.
It does not bring God closer.
It clears our vision.

From Waiting for God to Act to Growing Up in Christ

For many, prayer was shaped by waiting.

Waiting for God to move.
Waiting for God to arrive.
Waiting for heaven to open again.

That posture made sense in a theology of distance.
It does not fit the Gospel Jesus announces.

In Christ, God is not absent.
The heavens are not closed.
The Spirit is not withheld.
The Kingdom is not pending.

Prayer marks a shift from event-centred spirituality to maturity-centred formation.
This is not diminished prayer — it is grown-up prayer.

The New Testament assumes God's presence and directs its prayers toward human transformation:
eyes opened,
hearts strengthened,
minds renewed,
love embodied.

Prayer is not meant to keep believers dependent, anxious, or perpetually waiting for breakthrough.
It is meant to form sons and daughters — people who discern, love, and act in alignment with the Father's life already shared with them.

As union settles, prayer matures.
It becomes less about urgency and more about faithfulness.
Less about asking God to act and more about joining what He is already doing.

Prayer as Participation, Not Performance

Mature prayer is not passive.
It is participatory.

It listens as much as it speaks.
It notices rather than strives.
It responds rather than pleads.

Prayer is not a technique for control.
It is not a formula for outcomes.
It is not a performance to prove faith.

Prayer is communion.

To pray is to attend to truth.
To agree with love.
To allow fear to quiet.
To let reality shape response.

When prayer becomes anxious, transactional, or desperate, it has drifted from the Kingdom.
Not because God has withdrawn,
but because perception has narrowed.

The truest prayer is not louder words —
it is deeper trust.

Living Prayer in Ordinary Life

Prayer was never meant to be confined to formal moments, locations, or language.

"Pray without ceasing" does not mean constant speech.
It means constant awareness.

Prayer lives in:
attention while working,
honesty in conflict,
discernment in decision,
gratitude in provision,
trust in uncertainty.

To live prayerfully is not to speak more religiously.
It is to live more truthfully.

Prayer does not remove responsibility.
It deepens it.

Those who pray from union do not wait for heaven to fix the world.
They participate in its healing.

They do not ask God to arrive.
They learn to embody presence.

They do not plead for power.
They live from authority rooted in love.

Prayer, in the Kingdom, is not the cry of absence.
It is the language of presence.

And where prayer becomes alignment rather than persuasion,
fear loses urgency,
trust grows quietly,
and life begins to flow without strain.

From this place of communion, trust becomes possible — even in uncertainty.

Anchor Texts:
Matthew 6:9–13; John 11:41–42; Romans 8:26–27; 1 Thessalonians 5:17

Chapter 19 — Provision Without Anxiety

When prayer is no longer driven by anxiety, our relationship to provision begins to change.

Jesus speaks more about anxiety than almost any other emotional state.

Not because provision does not matter —
but because anxiety reveals what we believe about the source.

Anxiety assumes:
Scarcity at the centre.
Uncertainty in God.
Responsibility that cannot be carried.

Jesus does not shame anxiety.
He questions its assumptions.

"Why do you worry?"

Trust Does Not Eliminate Wisdom

Living without anxiety does not mean:

- passivity

- irresponsibility

- lack of planning

It means planning without fear.
Trust does not remove responsibility; it removes panic from responsibility.

We steward because life is valuable — not because it is fragile.
We work because participation matters — not because survival depends on it.

Jesus feeds people without interrogating faith.
He provides without preconditions.

Provision flows where trust replaces panic.

Anchor Texts:
Matthew 6:25–34; Philippians 4:6–7; Proverbs 21:5

Chapter 20 — Healing Without Blame

Jesus never treats sickness as moral failure.

He does not:

- interrogate belief
- assign guilt
- measure worthiness

Healing in the Kingdom is not a reward.
It is a sign.

A sign that life is breaking in.

Where Jesus goes, healing follows — not because people qualify, but because **God desires wholeness**.

God's Desire Is Healing

Throughout the Gospels, Jesus consistently reveals the heart of God as **toward healing**.

He heals because He wants to.
He heals because love moves toward suffering.
He heals because sickness is not part of God's design for human life.

We never see Jesus interpreting sickness as God's instructional strategy.
He never suggests that suffering is spiritually productive.
He never portrays sickness as a divine strategy.

When people come to Jesus for healing, His posture is consistently willing and compassionate.

"I am willing," He says — again and again.

Healing is not something Jesus negotiates with the Father.
It is something He reveals about the Father.

This does not mean healing is automatic.
It does mean healing is **always desired**.

Healing Is Not Transactional

Jesus heals:

- before repentance

- without theological correction

- outside religious approval

He does not require:

- sufficient faith

- correct doctrine

- emotional intensity

- moral achievement

This does not deny mystery or complexity.
It denies blame.

Fear-based healing theology harms people twice:
once through suffering,
and again through shame.

Jesus heals without accusation.

Desire Without Blame

Affirming God's desire to heal does *not* mean:

- every sickness has an immediate cure

- every prayer results in visible change

- every outcome can be explained

It means something far more important:

> **Sickness is never interpreted as God's refusal.**
> **Lack of healing is never read as personal failure.**
> **Suffering is never framed as divine punishment or distance.**

Jesus never withdraws compassion when healing does not occur.
He never distances Himself from those who remain unwell.

Presence does not disappear where healing is delayed.

Bodies Matter — Without Becoming Currency

Health matters.
Bodies matter.

But health is not currency.

Care for the body is cooperation with life —
not negotiation with God.

We seek healing because God loves life.
We trust God even when healing is incomplete.
And we refuse every theology that turns suffering into accusation.

In the Kingdom, **healing flows from love —** never from leverage.

Anchor Texts:
Matthew 8:1–3; John 9:1–3; Luke 5:12–13; Acts 10:38

Chapter 21 — Authority Without Domination

Jesus does not reject authority.
He redefines it.

"You know how rulers dominate.
Not so with you."

Authority in the Kingdom:

- liberates rather than controls

- serves rather than coerces

- protects rather than threatens

Jesus never overrides conscience.
Coercion produces submission, not discipleship.
He never forces belief.
He allows people to walk away.

Any authority that requires fear to function
is not Christlike authority.

Authority Exists for Maturity

Kingdom authority exists to:

- affirm identity

- cultivate discernment

- release people into agency

Not to manage behaviour through fear.

Where authority diminishes humanity,
it contradicts the God who became human.

Anchor Texts:
Matthew 20:25–28; Luke 10:19; John 13:14–15

Chapter 22 — Discernment, Conscience, and the Spirit's Voice

God does not guide by bypassing agency.
The Spirit does not erase humanity — He restores it.
Guidance that bypasses agency is not guidance; it is control.

Discernment is not:
blind obedience
suppressed intuition
silenced conscience

"The Spirit bears witness with our spirit."

Witness implies partnership.

How the Spirit Actually Leads

Fear pressures.
God invites.

Fear demands urgency.
God forms trust.

Fear insists on certainty.
God grows wisdom.

Discernment develops through:
relationship
practice
mistakes
learning to listen without panic

If something called "God's will" requires you to betray conscience, safety, or integrity — pause.

God's will is often misused to pressure compliance, silence questions, or spiritualise harm.

Jesus never guided people by overriding their agency, instincts, or moral clarity.

God's guidance never violates the humanity He healed.

Anchor Texts:
Romans 8:16; Galatians 5:16–25; Hebrews 5:14

Chapter 23 — Spiritual Warfare Reframed: Truth, Not Combat

Spiritual warfare has often been framed as cosmic aggression.

Jesus reframes it completely.

Darkness is not defeated by force.
It is displaced by light.

The real battle is not power against power —
it is truth against deception.

Authority Comes From Position, Not Striving

"You are seated with Christ."

Warfare is not fighting toward victory.
It is standing from it.

Prayer is not a combat technique.
It is agreement with reality.

Where identity is settled,
deception loses leverage.

Warfare ends where fear loses its authority.

This is why Jesus never teaches His disciples to fight darkness — only to stand in light.

Anchor Texts:
Ephesians 6:12–18; Colossians 2:15; John 1:5

Chapter 24 — Mission Without Threat

Jesus does not send people to bring God to the world.
He sends them because God is already there.

"We do not bring God to people.
God is already present — and has been all along."

Mission begins with nearness, not absence.
With attention, not anxiety.
With trust, not urgency.

Jesus never behaves as though the Father is missing from the world and needs to be delivered by Christians.
He speaks and acts as though God is already at work —
ahead of Him, beneath the surface, often unrecognised.

This changes everything.

Mission is not about transporting holiness into hostile territory.
It is about revealing what is already true.

Jesus sends His followers to notice, name, and participate in what God is already doing —
healing the sick, restoring dignity, confronting harm, and awakening trust.

Mission Is Witness, Not Control
A witness does not manufacture truth.
A witness does not manage outcomes.
A witness does not coerce response.

A witness tells the truth about what has been seen, heard, and encountered —
and then releases control.

Jesus never sends His followers to:
force belief
secure decisions
manage responses
threaten consequences

He sends them to:
heal
announce peace
tell the truth
embody love

This is why Jesus can send people without scripts, leverage, or contingency plans.
He trusts the Spirit more than technique.

The Great Commission Without Fear
The Great Commission has often been framed as an urgent rescue mission —
as though delay risks God's absence or humanity's abandonment.

Jesus does not commission panic.
He commissions formation.

"Go and make disciples," He says —
not converts, not arguments won, not numbers secured.

A disciple is not someone who agrees quickly.
A disciple is someone apprenticed into a way of life.

Jesus does not tell His followers to teach people how to avoid punishment.
He tells them to teach people how to live.

And He grounds the entire commission not in threat, but in presence:

"I am with you always."

This is not a reward for obedience.
It is the foundation mission stands on.

Evangelism as Awakening

Evangelism, in the way of Jesus, is not pressure.
It is not argument.
It is not threat.

It is awakening.

It is helping people recognise:
that God is nearer than they were told
that love is already extended
that truth is already pressing in

Jesus often names faith before people know they have it.
He heals before belief is articulated.
He welcomes before repentance is complete.

He does not wait for certainty to emerge before revealing the Father.
He reveals the Father so that trust can grow.

Mission, then, is not about crossing lines or closing deals.
It is about telling the truth about reality —
and trusting that truth, once seen, will do its work.

Fear is never the Gospel's engine.
Love is.

Where fear becomes the method, fear becomes the message —
no matter how accurate the words sound.

But where love is embodied, truth gains credibility.
And where truth is trusted, transformation follows without coercion.

Jesus never commissions fear.
He commissions His followers to bear witness —
with their words, their lives, and their love —
to a Kingdom already breaking in.

Anchor Texts:
John 5:17; Luke 10:1–9; Acts 17:27–28

Chapter 25 — The Church as Family, Not Hierarchy

The Church is not:
a control structure
a belief police
a spiritual ladder

It is a community of maturing sons and daughters.

Leadership exists to:
equip
protect
release
serve

Not to dominate or mediate God.

Where safety exists, transformation accelerates.

The Church flourishes when people:
grow in agency
hear God without intermediaries
live without fear
embody love in the world

The Church does not exist to protect itself.
It exists to witness to the Kingdom.

Wherever fear governs community, formation stalls.
Wherever love governs, the Kingdom becomes visible.

Anchor Texts:
Ephesians 4:11–16; 1 Peter 5:2–3; Romans 8:14–17

SECTION V - FORMATION WITHOUT FEAR

Becoming Whole, Human, and Free in Union with God

Chapter 26 — Formation Begins With Belonging

By this point, something has already shifted.

Formation no longer feels like pressure to improve or fear of falling short.
The constant internal monitoring begins to quiet.
The need to manage God's opinion loosens its grip.

When belonging is settled, formation changes its shape.

Growth stops being driven by anxiety and starts unfolding naturally.
Obedience becomes responsive rather than reactive.
Holiness begins to look less like effort and more like alignment.

Not because standards were lowered —
but because fear is no longer in charge.

When identity is secure, desire itself is reshaped.
People stop asking, *"Am I allowed?"*
and begin asking, *"What brings life?"*

This is how the Kingdom forms people.

Not as servants anxiously managing approval,
but as sons and daughters learning to live from home.

In this kind of formation:

- change is slower, but deeper

- repentance is gentler, but truer

- discipline becomes wisdom, not punishment

Nothing has to be forced.

Love does what fear never could.
It forms from the inside out.

And where belonging is no longer in question,
becoming like Jesus is not a demand to meet —
it is a life that emerges.

Anchor Texts:
Romans 8:15–17; 1 John 3:1–3; Matthew 3:16–17

Chapter 27 — The Body as Participant, Not Obstacle

Salvation is not escape from embodiment.
It is the healing of embodiment.

"The Word became flesh."

God did not save us *from* bodies.
He joined Himself *to* them.

The body is not spiritually neutral.
It remembers, protects, signals, and responds.

Formation that ignores the body becomes:
abstract
dissociative
unsafe

Jesus forms people in bodies.
The Incarnation itself declares the body a permanent site of God's work.

This means formation includes:
rest
food
movement
touch
rhythm
boundaries

These are not spiritual currency.
They are cooperation with life.

Ignoring the body does not make people holy.
It makes them fragile.

The body is not the problem.
It is the place God chose to dwell.

Anchor Texts:
John 1:14; Romans 12:1; 1 Corinthians 6:19–20

Chapter 28 — Desire Healed, Not Suppressed

Desire is not sin.
Distorted desire is.

Fear-based religion treats desire as dangerous and must therefore control it.
Jesus treats desire as truthful but misdirected.
Desire itself is not the enemy; distortion is.

"You will know the truth, and the truth will set you free."

Desire shaped by fear becomes compulsive.
Desire shaped by love becomes generous.

Transformation is not wanting less.
It is wanting rightly.

As identity stabilises:
addictions lose urgency
compulsions weaken
shame loosens its grip
love becomes natural

Punishment does not heal desire.
Truth does.

Jesus does not crush desire.
He restores it to its true object.

Anchor Texts:
John 8:32; Galatians 5:16–17; Psalm 37:4

Chapter 29 — Transformation Is Slow, Organic, and Real

Jesus never describes growth as instant or mechanical.

He speaks of:
seeds
soil
seasons
fruit

Formation takes time because:
trust takes time
trauma heals gradually
habits re-pattern slowly
safety precedes change

Speed is not a fruit of the Spirit.
Faithfulness is.

Systems that demand rapid transformation often bypass safety — and create hidden harm.

God is patient not because He is distant,
but because love is patient.

Formation is not linear.
Progress includes pauses, setbacks, and reorientation.

Nothing honest disqualifies growth.

Anchor Texts:
Mark 4:26–29; Philippians 1:6; Galatians 6:9

Chapter 30 — Practices as Alignment, Not Payment

Spiritual practices do not earn transformation.
They make space for it.

Prayer, Scripture, silence, community, generosity, rest —
these are not ladders to God.

They are anchors into reality.

"Abide in me."

Practices do not:
impress God
secure approval
measure spirituality

They keep us open to what is already true.
Practices do not create life; they make space for it.

When practices become pressure, they stop forming.
When they become performance, they stop healing.

Practices serve formation —
not fear.

Anchor Texts:
John 15:4–7; Psalm 1; 1 Timothy 4:7–8

Chapter 31 — Failure as Information, Not Disqualification

Jesus never shames failure.
He redeems it.

Failure reveals:
where fear still governs
where wounds remain
where formation is unfinished

Condemnation halts growth.
Curiosity restores it.

"There is now no condemnation."

Shame produces hiding.
Safety produces honesty.
Honesty produces change.

Failure does not mean you are backsliding.
It does mean something still needs attention, healing, or truth.

God does not withdraw in disappointment.
He remains present in process.

Anchor Texts:
Romans 8:1; Proverbs 24:16; Psalm 51:6

Chapter 32 — Sexuality, Covenant, and Consent

Sexuality is not shameful.
It is formative.

Desire shapes attachment, trust, and identity.

Jesus honours bodies.
He protects the vulnerable.
He never coerces.

Consent is non-negotiable.
Anything that overrides agency cannot be holy, regardless of religious framing.

Anything sexual without consent is not holy.
It is harm.

Covenant is not control.
It is safety.

Marriage is mutual self-giving — not ownership.
Singleness is not deficiency.
Both are full participation.

Holiness heals distorted desire.
It does not erase desire itself.

Anchor Texts:
1 Corinthians 13; 1 Thessalonians 4:3–8; Song of Songs 2:7

Chapter 33 — Trauma, Truth, and Responsibility

A restorative theology must never minimise harm.

Jesus' mercy toward sinners never comes at the expense of the wounded.

Trauma is not sin.
It is injury.

Jesus restores safety before demanding change.

"He will not break a bruised reed."

Healing requires:
time
truth
boundaries
consent
care

Union does not bypass the nervous system.
Responsibility remains real — without shame.

Harm is named.
Repair is pursued.
Patterns are confronted.

Restoration is not soft.
It is exacting — because it refuses denial.

Anchor Texts:
Isaiah 42:3; Luke 4:18; John 8:31–32

Chapter 34 — Boundaries, Authority, and Spiritual Abuse

Spiritual abuse thrives where silence is spiritualised.

Abuse is not misunderstanding.
Coercion is not discipleship.
Control is not authority.

Jesus:
refuses domination
rejects forced submission
allows people to leave
confronts leaders who burden others

Submission in Scripture is mutual — never blind.
Any theology that demands silence in the face of harm has already left Jesus behind.

Boundaries are not unloving.
They are conditions for safety.

Leaving a harmful system is sometimes faithfulness.
Endurance is not holiness when harm continues.

The Kingdom restores agency.
It does not consume it.

Agency is the God-given capacity to perceive, choose, and respond freely.
Love does not override agency — it requires it.

Anchor Texts:
Matthew 23:4; Galatians 2:11–14; Ephesians 5:21

Chapter 35 — Unity Without Coercion

Unity is not sameness.
The body has many parts because difference is design.

Jesus never imagines unity as uniformity.
He speaks of a body precisely because bodies require difference to live.
Hands are not feet.
Eyes are not ears.
Life depends on distinction, not its erasure.

When unity is defined as sameness, difference becomes a threat.
When difference becomes a threat, control soon follows.

Disagreement is not danger.
Silencing conscience is.

Jesus does not fear questions, hesitation, or dissent.
He engages disagreement without panic.
He corrects without humiliation.
He allows people to wrestle, misunderstand, and even walk away.

What He consistently resists is not disagreement —
but coercion disguised as faithfulness.

Truth does not need control to survive.

If something must be enforced to remain believable,
it is already fragile.

Truth can be examined.
Love can be questioned.
Reality does not collapse under scrutiny.

Unity deepens where love is strong enough to hold difference.
It fractures where fear demands uniformity.

Fear-driven unity relies on pressure, silence, and spiritualised conformity.
It calls suppression "peace" and avoidance "maturity."
But peace built on fear is not peace — it is containment.

Love-driven unity is slower.
It allows tension without threat.
It makes room for growth, change, and honest speech.

This kind of unity does not require everyone to think the same way at the same time.
It requires people to remain present, truthful, and committed to one another's good.

The Kingdom is held together by love —
not agreement.

Jesus does not pray that His followers would all say the same things.
He prays that they would be one as He and the Father are one.

Their oneness is not sameness of thought.
It is shared life, shared love, and shared participation.

Unity in the Kingdom is not enforced from the outside.
It emerges from the inside —
as people remain rooted in love rather than fear.

Anchor Texts:
1 Corinthians 12; John 17:20–23; Romans 14

Chapter 36 — Children, Parenting, and Formation

Children are not born separated from God.
The Kingdom already belongs to them.

Jesus does not speak of children as future participants in God's life —
waiting to mature, repent, or believe correctly.
He names them as present participants.

When His disciples attempt to keep children away, Jesus is indignant.
He does not tolerate their exclusion, delay, or management.

"Let the little children come to Me, and do not hinder them," He says,
"for to such belongs the Kingdom of God."

He does not say the Kingdom *will belong* to them one day.
He says it *already does*.

Jesus does not require belief statements from children.
He does not warn them about sin, judgment, or hell.
He does not frame them as morally suspect or spiritually dangerous.

Instead, He receives them.
He blesses them.
He places them at the centre and tells adults to learn from them.

In doing so, Jesus reveals something foundational:
children are not problems to be fixed —
they are lives already held within God's care.

Children are not born as sinners in need of condemnation.
They are born human — alive, forming, learning, and deeply receptive.

Sin, as Jesus reveals it, is not an inherited stain carried at birth.
It is learned distortion.
Misbelief.
Fear absorbed over time.

To name children as "sinners" before they can even speak is not biblical formation —
it is fear projected onto innocence.

Belonging precedes belief.
Safety precedes formation.

Before a child can discern truth, they must experience trust.
Before they can interpret God rightly, they must encounter love embodied consistently around them.

Formation that begins with fear may produce outward compliance,
but it does not produce wisdom, courage, or resilient faith.

Love-based formation does.

Discipline, in the way of Jesus, is guidance — not punishment.
It is direction offered from relationship, not correction imposed from threat.
Its purpose is not control, but clarity.
Not shame, but growth.

Children learn theology long before they learn language.
Tone teaches before words do.
Presence shapes belief more deeply than instruction.

A God introduced through fear will be internalised as unsafe.
A faith formed through threat will eventually fracture — either into anxiety or rejection.

Hell-based fear damages the nervous system before it ever forms character.

It trains vigilance, not trust.
Compliance, not discernment.

Trust, by contrast, forms resilient faith.
It allows children to ask real questions, tell the truth about their inner world, and grow without hiding.

So we teach love.
We teach discernment.
We teach courage.

We teach children that God is near, kind, and trustworthy —
even when life is hard,
even when mistakes are made,
even when answers are not clear.

Children flourish where God is safe.
And where God is safe, formation unfolds naturally —
not as pressure to perform,
but as a life learned in love.

Anchor Texts:
Mark 10:13–16; Matthew 18:1–6; Psalm 127

Chapter 37 — Lament, Grief, and Protest

Lament is not unbelief.
It is love refusing denial.

Lament begins where pretending ends.
It names the ache rather than hiding it.
It speaks because silence would be a lie.

Jesus lamented.
The Psalms protest.
God listens.

Scripture does not censor grief.
It preserves it.

"Why have You forsaken Me?"
— spoken by Love incarnate.

Jesus does not sanitise suffering in His darkest hour.
He prays it.
He brings unanswered pain directly into relationship.

God does not require emotional editing.

He does not ask us to sound strong, resolved, or certain when we are not.

Honest grief is prayer.

Tears are not a failure of faith.
They are often its most truthful language.

Protest says:
"This is not right — and I believe You care."

To protest is not to accuse God of absence.
It is to appeal to His goodness.
It is to hold God to who He has revealed Himself to be.

Silence is not holiness.

Silence may protect others' comfort,
but it does not protect truth.

Holiness does not demand the suppression of pain.
It sanctifies the courage to name it.

Truth spoken in grief is faith.

Faith does not mean explaining suffering away.
It means refusing to abandon relationship inside it.

The Kingdom does not rush people past pain.

It does not offer bypasses, platitudes, or timelines.

It stays present inside pain —
bearing witness, sharing breath, and holding space
until healing can actually begin.

This is the posture of God.
Not distant.
Not hurried.
But near enough to weep.

Lament is what love sounds like when it refuses to pretend.

Anchor Texts:
Psalm 13; Psalm 88; Matthew 27:46; Romans 8:26

SECTION VI - WHEN FEAR-BASED FAITH FALLS APART

Deconstruction, Reconstruction, and Finding Jesus Again

Chapter 38 — When Faith Unravels, It Is Often Maturing

For many, faith does not collapse because it is weak.
It collapses because it has grown strong enough to refuse distortion.

Often, people do not set out to deconstruct anything.
They simply reach a point where something no longer fits —
where the cost of staying silent becomes higher than the cost of asking questions.

Most people do not deconstruct because they want less God.
They deconstruct because they want God without fear.

But many do not yet have language for this.
They do not think, *"This is distortion."*
They think, *"Something is wrong — and I don't know why."*

Fear-based faith is often inherited before it is examined.
It feels normal because it is familiar.
It only becomes visible when it begins to harm.

Common catalysts include:

- a God who feels volatile, distant, or unsafe

- hell doctrines that damage the nervous system rather than produce love

- authority structures that override conscience in the name of obedience

- discovering Scripture does not say what they were told it says recognising that Jesus does not behave like the system built around Him

Often, the first sign of distortion is not intellectual doubt,
but emotional dissonance.

Prayer becomes anxious.
Worship feels performative.
Scripture triggers fear instead of trust.
Belief requires constant vigilance rather than rest.

People begin to feel that faith demands shrinking —
less honesty, less agency, less humanity.

When a belief system cannot survive honesty,
it was never meant to carry the weight of truth.

This is not rebellion.
It is discernment awakening.

Loss of certainty is not loss of faith.
Certainty and faith are not the same thing.

Certainty seeks control.
Faith learns trust.

Faith matures when it no longer needs fear to function.

Mature faith can live with mystery.
It can ask without panic.
It can release false images of God without losing God Himself.

What unravels in deconstruction is often not faith —
but fear dressed up as faith.

And when fear loosens its grip,
what remains is not emptiness,
but a deeper capacity for love, truth, and trust.

Anchor Texts:
Hebrews 5:14; Mark 9:24; John 8:32

Chapter 39 — You Are Not Backsliding — You Are Waking Up

Deconstruction often feels like regression — but it isn't.

It commonly includes:

- anxiety and relief at the same time
- grief over what once felt secure
- anger at manipulation
- fear of "going too far"
- loneliness without a map

This is not spiritual danger.
It is the nervous system recalibrating after prolonged pressure.
Danger comes from denial, not honesty.

When faith has been held together by fear,
movement will initially feel like collapse.

Fear mistakes movement for threat.
Love recognises awakening.

You are allowed to pause.

You are allowed to not know.

You are allowed to cry for what you lost,
even if it once sustained you.

You are allowed to feel anger at what was manipulative,
without becoming bitter or unloving.

You are allowed to rant, question, protest, and grieve —
without rushing to resolve the tension.

You are allowed to hold loss and freedom at the same time.

Healing is not tidy.
Awakening is not linear.

Strong emotions do not mean you are doing something wrong.
They mean something real is being released.

God is not measuring your progress during this season.

He is not keeping score, tracking certainty, or timing recovery.

He is staying present inside it —
patient, non-anxious, and near.

Anchor Texts:
Psalm 34:18; Matthew 11:28–30; John 20:24–29

Chapter 40 — Grieving What You Are Losing

Deconstruction includes real loss.

You may be losing:

- a God who felt predictable

- a community that once felt safe

- simple answers

- clear boundaries of "in" and "out"

- certainty that made life manageable

Grief does not mean you are failing spiritually.
It means something mattered enough to be mourned.

Do not rush grief to reach clarity.
Clarity emerges after safety returns.

God does not hurry mourning.
Jesus wept even when resurrection was minutes away.

Grief is not the enemy of faith.
Avoiding grief is.

Anchor Texts:
John 11:33–35; Psalm 42; Ecclesiastes 3:1–4

Chapter 41 — Jesus Is Not What Is Being Deconstructed

What usually collapses is not Jesus.

It is what was placed on top of Him.

Fear-based systems trained people to confuse Jesus with:

- institutional power

- control mechanisms

- threat-based salvation

- behaviour management

- certainty addiction

Deconstruction often reveals this simple truth:

"I did not lose Jesus.
I lost what was attached to Him."

Jesus survives every honest question.
Systems rarely do.

When something collapses as fear loosens, it often reveals what was doing the holding.

Anchor Texts:
Matthew 15:8–9; John 6:68; Luke 24:32

Chapter 42 — If Faith Only Worked Through Fear, It Was Never Free

Fear can produce:

- compliance

- behaviour modification

- moral performance

Fear cannot produce:

- love

- trust

- union

- transformation

Perfect love casts out fear —
not perfect theology.

If removing fear causes faith to collapse,
fear was the foundation, not love.
Many inherited this sincerely — without malicious intent.

Love never needed intimidation to exist.

Faith that only survives under threat is not faith.
It is survival.

Jesus never built faith that way.

Anchor Texts:
1 John 4:18; Romans 8:15; Galatians 5:1

Chapter 43 — Jesus Is Often Found in the Wreckage

Many discover something unexpected during deconstruction.

Prayer becomes more honest.
Scripture becomes alive again.
God feels closer, not farther.
Compassion deepens.
Shame loosens.

This can feel disorienting.

People expect distance from God —
but instead, they encounter presence.

This is because deconstruction is often misunderstood.

Deconstruction is not the destruction of faith.
It is the dismantling of what was never faith to begin with.

It is the slow collapse of fear-based images of God.
The unlearning of control disguised as holiness.
The exposure of beliefs that required suppression, silence, or anxiety to survive.

When those structures fall,
many expect emptiness.

Instead, they find Christ.

This is not drifting from Jesus.
It is often returning to Him without fear.

Jesus is not identical to the systems built around Him.
He is not confined to inherited frameworks, certainty structures, or religious machinery.

In the Gospels, Jesus is consistently found *outside* the places people expect Him —
at tables rather than temples,
with the wounded rather than the certain,
in questions rather than answers.

So when systems collapse,
it does not mean Christ has left.

It often means the noise has quieted enough
for Him to be seen again.

Jesus is not offended by your questions.
He is revealed through them.

Questions do not threaten truth.
They threaten control.

Jesus never demands certainty as the price of relationship.
He meets people in confusion, grief, doubt, and discovery —
and calls them by name there.

What is falling apart may be the distortion —
not the relationship.

Many realise that what they were defending was not Christ,
but a version of faith held together by fear.

When fear loosens,
what remains is often simpler, truer, and more alive.

Faith becomes less about managing belief
and more about trust.

Less about being right
and more about being honest.

Less about protecting God
and more about recognising Him.

Jesus is often found in the wreckage
because He was never in the machinery.

He was in the margins.
In the questions.
In the wounds.
In the honest cry that refused to pretend.

Deconstruction does not mean Jesus is gone.
It often means He is finally visible —
unobscured by fear.

Anchor Texts:
Luke 5:1–11; John 21; Luke 19:1–10

Chapter 44 — Reconstruction Without Panic

Reconstruction is not architectural.
It is relational.

It is not the urgent rebuilding of a belief system
to replace the one that collapsed.
It is the slow reorientation of trust —
learning again how to relate to God without fear.

After deconstruction, many feel pressure to *reconstruct quickly*.
To land somewhere.
To regain clarity.
To prove they are still "okay."

But faith rebuilt in panic
will eventually demand panic to survive.

You do not need to rebuild everything at once.

You are allowed to say:
"I don't know yet."

You are allowed to say:
"I'm holding this loosely."

You are allowed to say:
"I trust God more than my conclusions."

These are not evasions.
They are signs of humility and maturity.

Urgency is rarely from God.
It is usually fear trying to regain control.

Fear rushes because it cannot tolerate uncertainty.
Love waits because it trusts presence.

God is not anxious about where you will land.

He is not standing on the other side of your questions
waiting for you to arrive at the correct position.

He is already with you —
inside the not-knowing,
inside the re-learning,
inside the slow forming of trust.

Reconstruction is not about certainty returning.
It is about safety returning.

As fear loosens,
truth can be approached without defence.
Scripture can be read without panic.
Community can be entered without performance.

What emerges is often simpler than what was lost.

Not a system to defend,
but a relationship to live.

Not answers to guard,
but a presence to trust.

Reconstruction happens at the speed of trust.

And trust cannot be forced.
It grows as love proves itself patient, consistent, and near.

This is not stalled faith.
It is faith learning to breathe again.

Anchor Texts:
Proverbs 3:5–6; Psalm 127:1; John 14:1

Chapter 45 — Start With Jesus, Not Answers

Reconstruction does not begin with doctrines.
It begins with orientation.

Before asking, *"What do I believe now?"*
Jesus invites a different question:
"Who do you see when you look at Me?"

Start there.

Ask:
How does Jesus treat people?
How does He respond to fear-based religion?
Where does He refuse coercion?
Who does He protect?

When religious leaders bring Him a woman caught in adultery,
Jesus does not defend the system that exposed her.
He protects her from violence, disarms her accusers,
and restores her dignity before addressing her life.

When the Sabbath is weaponised against healing,
Jesus does not prioritise doctrinal correctness.
He heals anyway — and asks whether law was ever meant to harm.

When Peter denies Him,
Jesus does not revoke his calling.
He restores him with breakfast, questions of love, and trust.

When Thomas doubts,
Jesus does not shame him for uncertainty.
He invites him closer.

When crowds walk away because His teaching is difficult,
Jesus does not chase them with clarification or threat.
He lets them go.

This is the posture of God.

Jesus interprets Scripture.
Scripture does not domesticate Jesus.

When readings of the Bible contradict the compassion, freedom, and non-coercive love of Christ,
Jesus does not need to be adjusted to fit them.
They need to be reread through Him.

If a belief makes Jesus less loving,
less human,
or less trustworthy — pause.

If it requires fear to function,
coercion to survive,
or silence to remain unquestioned — pause.

Truth will never require you to betray the character of Christ.

Reconstruction becomes dangerous
when people start with answers and then try to force Jesus to agree with them.

It becomes life-giving
when people stay oriented toward Him
and let conclusions form slowly in His presence.

You do not need to solve everything.
You need to keep looking at Jesus.

Not the abstract Christ of systems,
but the living Christ of the Gospels —
who touches the unclean,
eats with the excluded,

challenges the powerful,
and refuses to control belief.

This is not avoidance.
It is fidelity.

Reconstruction that begins with Jesus
may feel slower,
but it will be truer.

And it will always lead you toward
love without fear,
truth without coercion,
and faith that can finally breathe.

Anchor Texts:
John 8:1–11; John 20:24–29; John 21:15–19

Chapter 46 — Beware of Replacing One Certainty With Another

Those leaving rigid systems are vulnerable.

When certainty collapses, the nervous system looks for something solid.
Something to stand on.
Something to end the ambiguity.

This is understandable — and dangerous.

It is tempting to replace:

old certainty → new certainty

old control → reverse control

old dogma → new dogma

The labels change.
The posture stays the same.

Reconstruction can quietly become another form of defence —
not against fear-based religion this time,
but against uncertainty itself.

This is how fear sneaks back in.

It sounds like:
"I finally see clearly now."
"This is the correct framework."
"Anyone who disagrees just isn't awake yet."

When certainty returns too quickly,
it is often fear trying to regain control —
not truth settling in.

Reconstruction is not about being *right again*.
It is about learning to live without fear.

Truth does not need immediacy.
Wisdom grows in patience.

Faith that has been healed does not rush to land.
It can hold questions without turning them into conclusions.
It can speak convictions without weaponising them.

How to recognise when fear is rebuilding:

- when disagreement feels threatening again

- when curiosity is replaced by certainty

- when identity depends on being "on the right side"

- when belonging requires agreement

How to recognise when trust is growing:

- when you can say "I might be wrong" without panic

- when you remain open even while holding convictions

- when love matters more than being correct

- when Jesus remains central, not your framework

You do not need to arrive anywhere to be faithful.

Faithfulness is not a destination.
It is a posture.

It looks like staying honest.
Staying relational.
Staying oriented toward Jesus rather than conclusions.

Reconstruction that remains free
does not eliminate beliefs —
it loosens the grip they have on identity.

What emerges is not vagueness,
but humility.

Not endless uncertainty,
but trust.

The goal is not to replace one certainty with another,
The goal is to become safe enough to live without fear.

That is not weakness.

It is maturity.

Anchor Texts:
1 Corinthians 8:1–3; James 3:17; Philippians 3:7–8

Chapter 47 — Guidance for Pastors, Leaders, and Companions

People rarely deconstruct because they are rebellious, lazy, or careless with truth.

More often, they deconstruct because something inside them can no longer cooperate with fear.

Their nervous system no longer feels safe.
Their conscience refuses to be silenced.
Their soul is tired of pretending everything is fine when it is not.

Deconstruction is not usually an intellectual revolt.
It is a physiological and spiritual response to prolonged misalignment.

The role of leaders in these moments is not correction.
It is safety.

Before clarity can emerge, fear must settle.
Before truth can be heard, the body must feel protected.
Before formation can continue, trust must be restored.

Leaders do not serve people in deconstruction by:

- defending systems that harmed them

- closing questions too quickly

- rushing people toward conclusions they are not ready to hold

- treating doubt as danger

These responses may preserve structures,
but they do not preserve souls.

What leaders are called to do instead is quieter — and harder.

They regulate fear rather than escalate it.
They hold space rather than fill it with answers.
They normalise doubt without celebrating cynicism.
They protect Jesus from distortion — not by argument, but by presence.

To lead well here is to resist the urge to fix.
It is to listen without agenda.
To stay when outcomes are unclear.
To trust that God is not threatened by honest questioning.

Jesus never argued people back into safety.
He embodied it.

He allowed confusion without shaming it.
He met people in their fear without amplifying it.
He told the truth without panic.
And He trusted that love, once felt, would do what pressure never could.

Pastors and leaders are not called to manage people back into belief.
They are called to walk with them until trust becomes possible again.

This requires patience.
It requires humility.
It requires a willingness to let go of control.

But it is here — in safety, honesty, and unforced presence —
that faith either heals or finally rests.

And when leaders choose safety over certainty,
they do more than retain people.

They reveal Jesus.

Anchor Texts:
Matthew 11:28–30; John 20:19–22; Luke 24:36–45; Isaiah 42:3

Chapter 48 — Losing Christianity Is Not Losing Christ

Christianity is a tradition.
Jesus is a person.

Many are not losing Christ —
they are losing a version of Christianity He never endorsed.

What often falls away is:

- fear

- shame

- control

- performance

- exclusion

What remains is:

- love

- trust

- presence

- union

- freedom

God is not standing at the edge of your questions.
He has always been present within them.

Anchor Texts:
John 6:66–69; Hebrews 13:8; Matthew 28:20

Chapter 49 — What to Hold Onto When Everything Feels Uncertain

You do not need all the answers.

When certainty dissolves, the instinct is to replace it quickly —
to grasp for explanations, frameworks, or conclusions that promise relief.

But faith does not require answers to survive.
It requires orientation.

When everything feels uncertain, hold onto what is relational, not conceptual.

Hold onto **Jesus** —
not as an idea to define,
but as a person to keep returning to.

Read the Gospels slowly.
Notice how He treats people.
Let His posture shape yours before His words become doctrines.

If your faith still looks like Jesus,
you are not lost.

Hold onto **love**.

When you are unsure what to believe,
choose the most loving action available to you.

Love is not vague.
It looks like kindness, patience, protection of the vulnerable, and refusal to harm.
Love is never the wrong direction.

Hold onto **honesty**.

Say what is actually true —
to God, to yourself, to safe people.

"I don't know."
"I'm confused."
"I'm angry."
"I'm grieving."

These are not failures of faith.
They are the ground where real faith grows.

Hold onto **humility**.

You are allowed to hold convictions without hardening them into identity.
You are allowed to be wrong without collapsing.

Humility keeps faith flexible, curious, and human.

Hold onto **curiosity**.

Ask questions without rushing to answer them.
Stay interested rather than defensive.

Curiosity is often the sign that fear is loosening its grip.

Hold onto **compassion** —
especially for yourself.

You are learning to breathe in a new way.
That takes time.

If your faith journey has become gentler,
more honest,
and more human,
it is likely becoming truer — not weaker.

What to Let Go Of

Let go of **fear-based urgency**.

You do not need to figure everything out now.
God is not in a hurry.

Let go of **performative certainty**.

You do not owe anyone a finished theology.
Faith is not proven by confidence.

Let go of **spiritual superiority**.

Awakening is not elevation above others.
It is deepening into love.

Let go of **threat-driven belief**.

Any belief that requires fear to hold it together
is not yet healed.

Faith is not certainty.
Faith is trust.

And trust grows where safety exists —
where God is not volatile,
questions are allowed,
and love remains the measure.

If you can stay oriented toward Jesus,
choose love when unsure,
and remain honest rather than afraid,

you are holding onto exactly what matters.

Everything else can form in time.

Anchor Texts:
Micah 6:8; 1 Corinthians 13; John 15:9–12

Chapter 50 — When You Fear You Might Be Wrong

God is not waiting to punish honesty.

You are allowed to:

- be wrong

- change your mind

- grow slowly

- learn in public or private

Truth does not fear patience.

If God is love,
He is not threatened by your questions.

Anchor Texts:
Psalm 25:4–5; Romans 14:4; John 16:13

Chapter 51 — You Are Not Losing Truth — You Are Losing Fear

If you are deconstructing:
you are not broken
you are not rebellious
you are not faithless
you are not alone

If something false is falling apart,
it is making room for something true.

You are not losing Jesus.
You are seeing Him without fear.

Truth does not disappear when fear does. It becomes clearer.

Anchor Texts:
2 Timothy 1:7; John 18:37; 1 John 4:16

SECTION VII - THE STORY WE LIVE INSIDE

A Jesus-Shaped Gospel for the World

Chapter 52 — The Story Is Not About Escape — It Is About Healing

Many inherited a story shaped like this:

Humanity failed.
God became angry.
Jesus intervened.
Some people escape.
The rest are lost.

Jesus tells a different story.

The biblical story is not about evacuation from a doomed world.
It is about God refusing to abandon creation to death, fear, and fracture.

From beginning to end, Scripture moves toward:

- healing, not abandonment

- restoration, not replacement

- union, not separation

The Gospel is not a rescue plan *from* God.
It is the revelation that God has never left.

Jesus does not arrive to save us from creation.
He arrives to save creation *from death* — by joining it.

This is the story resurrection tells — and it is the story creation has been waiting for.

Anchor Texts:
John 1:14; Romans 8:19–23; Colossians 1:15–20

Chapter 53 — The World Is Not God-Forsaken — It Is God-Haunted

Jesus does not announce a God who might arrive someday. He announces a Kingdom already near, already present, already pressing in.

"The Kingdom of God is among you."

This means:

- no place is God-absent

- no person is beyond divine reach

- no culture is spiritually empty

Mission is not bringing God somewhere He is missing.
It is unveiling the God who is already there.

The world is not abandoned.
It is saturated.

Grace is not scarce.
Presence is not withheld.

The world groans not because God is absent,

but because His restoring presence is being resisted, opposed, and awaited.

Anchor Texts:
Acts 17:27–28; Psalm 139; John 5:17

Chapter 54 — The Kingdom Is Not a Place — It Is a Way of Being

The Kingdom is not:

- a future location

- a religious institution

- a political empire

The Kingdom is God's life made visible.
It is not abstract spirituality — it is life lived in love, truth, and restoration.

It appears wherever:

- love replaces fear

- truth replaces lies

- healing replaces harm

- dignity replaces domination

Jesus does not ask people to wait for the Kingdom.
He invites them to live from it.

The Kingdom is not imposed.
It is embodied.

It grows quietly — like yeast, like seed, like light.

Anchor Texts:
Luke 17:20–21; Matthew 13; Romans 14:17

Chapter 55 — What This Gospel Forms in People

A fear-based gospel forms anxious people.

It produces:

- performance

- dependence on authority

- fear of exclusion

- certainty addiction

A Jesus-centred Gospel forms grounded people.

It produces:

- courage without coercion

- honesty without panic

- compassion without superiority

- agency without isolation

This Gospel forms people who:

- are not easily manipulated

- do not need enemies

- protect the vulnerable

- tell the truth without violence

The fruit of the Gospel is not correct belief alone.
Correct belief matters — but it is meant to *serve* transformation, not replace it.

Anchor Texts:
Matthew 7:16–20; Galatians 5:22–23; James 1:22

Chapter 56 — The Church as a Community of the Healed and Healing

The Church is not defined by control, sorting, or gatekeeping — those stories have already been told.

The Church is a community learning to live from union.

Its calling is not to manage sin.
It is to nurture maturity.

Authority in the Church exists to:
serve growth
protect dignity
release people into freedom

Authority does not replace discernment.
It creates safety for discernment to grow.

The Church succeeds when people:
grow in agency
hear God without intermediaries
live without fear
embody love in the world

Formation deepens where people are trusted to mature rather than managed to comply.

The Church does not exist to preserve itself.
It exists to bear witness to the Kingdom —
not by enforcing belief,
but by embodying a life where love is credible, freedom is protected, and truth heals.

Anchor Texts:
Ephesians 4:11–16; Acts 2:42–47; John 13:34–35

Chapter 57 — Power, Politics, and the Way of Jesus

Jesus does not reject power.
He redefines it.

Power in the Kingdom:

- does not dominate

- does not coerce

- does not demand allegiance through fear

Jesus exercises power by:

- serving

- healing

- forgiving

- refusing violence

The Kingdom does not advance through force.
It advances through truth embodied in love.

Any system that requires fear to survive
is not aligned with the way of Jesus.

Anchor Texts:
Matthew 20:25–28; John 18:36; Philippians 2:5–11

Chapter 58 — Judgment, Hope, and the Refusal to Abandon Anyone

Judgment is not the end of the story.
It is truth revealed so healing can occur.

The biblical trajectory moves toward:

- purification, not perpetual punishment

- restoration, not eternal exclusion

- reconciliation, not abandonment

God's judgment does not compete with mercy.
It is mercy refusing illusion.

The final word spoken over creation is not condemnation.
It is renewal.

Love does not give up.
Truth does not fail.
God does not abandon

Anchor Texts:
Lamentations 3:31–33; Psalm 96:13; John 12:47–48

Chapter 59 — Death Is Not the Final Horizon

Christian hope is not disembodied escape.
It is resurrection.

The Gospel does not point us away from creation.
It points us toward its healing.

From the beginning, God's commitment has not been to rescue souls *from* the world,
but to restore the world *through* love.

The future is not:
souls floating away
creation discarded
history abandoned

God does not abandon what He called "very good."

The future is:
renewed bodies
healed creation
God dwelling with humanity

Resurrection is not the survival of the soul alone.
It is the renewal of the whole person.

Jesus does not rise as a ghost.
He rises embodied.
Wounded, recognisable, transformed.

In Him, God reveals not only who He is,
but what humanity — and creation — are destined to become.

This matters.

If the future were escape,
bodies would not matter.
Justice would not matter.
Creation would not matter.

But resurrection says:
what is done in love is not lost.
what is suffered is not ignored.
what is broken is not discarded.

Death does not end God's work.

It interrupts our sight —
but not God's faithfulness.

Judgment does not destroy hope.

Judgment is not God turning against creation,
but God telling the truth about it —
exposing what deforms, heals what is wounded,
and refining what cannot endure love.

Judgment is not the opposite of mercy.
It is mercy refusing to leave anything unhealed.

Love completes what it begins.

God does not abandon people midway through transformation.
He does not create, incarnate, heal, and restore —
only to stop at death.

The arc of God's work bends toward life.

Not abstract life.
Embodied life.
Shared life.
Life where God dwells with humanity,
and creation finally rests from its groaning.

This is not naïve optimism.
It is resurrection hope.

And resurrection means:
death is not the final horizon —
love is.

Anchor Texts:
1 Corinthians 15; John 11:25–26; Revelation 21:1–5

Chapter 60 — Living the Age to Come Now

Eternal life is not postponed.
It begins now.

Eternal life is:

- knowing God

- living from union

- participating in restoration

- embodying love without fear

The Church does not wait for the future.
It rehearses it.

Every act of healing, justice, mercy, and courage
is a preview of what is coming.

The Kingdom is not someday.
It is already breaking in.

Anchor Texts:
John 17:3; 2 Corinthians 5:17; Hebrews 6:4–5

Chapter 61 — The Final Shape of the Gospel

This Gospel proclaims:

God is not against you.
God is not distant.
God is not fragile.
God is not violent.

God is revealed in Jesus.

Jesus reveals:

- who God has always been

- who humanity truly is

- what the world is becoming

The Good News is not that God will tolerate you if you believe correctly.

The Good News is that God has united Himself to humanity —
and invites us to wake up, trust, and live from that truth.

Anchor Texts:
Colossians 1:27; Ephesians 1:9–10; John 1:9

FINAL DECLARATION — The Story We Live Inside

We do not live inside a story of fear.
We live inside a story where:
love precedes repentance
belonging precedes belief
healing precedes holiness
union precedes transformation

We live inside a story where God is not distant, volatile, or waiting to be convinced.

From the beginning, creation was not a test — it was a gift.
Not a proving ground — a home.

Humanity was not created broken and dangerous,
but bearing the image and likeness of God —
designed to reflect, carry, and participate in divine life.

There was no original distance to overcome.
No suspicion to manage.
No wrath hiding beneath love.

The fracture in the human story was not rebellion first —
it was forgetting.
Forgetting who God is.
Forgetting who we are.
Forgetting that life flows from trust, not control.

And from that forgetting came fear.
From fear came hiding.
From hiding came violence, domination, religion, hierarchy, and blame.

But God did not withdraw.

The story of Scripture is not humanity searching for God —
it is God refusing to abandon humanity.

Again and again, through prophets and poets, through exile and return,
God keeps saying the same thing in different ways:
"I am with you."
"You are still mine."
"I have not left."

And then God stopped speaking about Himself —
and showed up.

Jesus does not absorb wrath so the Father can finally love.
He reveals that the Father has always been like Him.

In Him we see:
God touching the unclean
God forgiving without leverage
God restoring dignity before behaviour changes
God choosing mercy over control
God standing with the wounded, not the powerful

There is no second face behind Jesus.
No hidden wrath.
No cosmic split.

The cross is not God against humanity.
 It is love against the lie.

It is what happens when perfect love enters a violent system —
and refuses to become violent in return.

On the cross, God forgives while being murdered.
God absorbs fear without retaliation.
God enters death to heal it from the inside.

The cross is not payment.
It is revelation.
"This is what God is like — even when you kill Him."

And the resurrection declares that love was telling the truth.

Death does not get the final word.
Separation does not win.
Union is stronger than the grave.

Jesus rises not as an exception,
but as the beginning of a healed humanity.

And He does not ascend to leave us behind.
He sends the Spirit to live within us.

God is not distant.
God is not external.
God is not waiting.

God has joined Himself to humanity — permanently.

Salvation, then, is not escape from the world.
It is awakening inside it.

Repentance is not grovelling.
It is waking up.

Faith is not pressure to believe the right things.
It is learning to trust what has always been true.

The Kingdom is not postponed.
It is present.

Judgment is not love failing.
It is love refusing to lie.

Fire does not exist to torture.
It exists to heal, refine, and reveal.

Hell is not God's final word.
Restoration is.

**This is not because God bypasses human agency,
but because God's faithfulness does not abandon what He has
joined to Himself.**

The story does not end with abandonment, division, or escape.
It ends with homecoming.

Heaven and earth reunited.
Humanity healed.
Creation restored.

"Behold, I am making all things new."
Not some things.
All things.

This is not optimism.
This is resurrection faith.

This is the Gospel.
And it is the story you are already inside.

You are not trying to reach God.
You are learning to trust that God has already reached you.

You are not becoming loved.
You are waking up to love.

So live from it.
Rest in it.
Let fear loosen its grip.
Let love tell the truth.

This is the Good News.
And it has always been GOOD.

And where this Gospel is trusted, fear loosens, love grows, and life begins to heal.

APPENDIX A — FEAR-BASED VS UNION-BASED CHRISTIANITY

A Side-by-Side Discernment Tool

This contrast describes postures, not people.

Fear-Based Framework	Union-Based Framework
Motivation: Threat	Motivation: Love
Behaviour control	Desire healing
God is distant	God is present
Faith equals certainty	Faith equals trust
Compliance valued	Maturity cultivated
Shame enforces change	Truth transforms

Control preserves unity   Love sustains unity

Discernment question:

Use these questions slowly and honestly.
They are not tests of correctness, but guides toward health.

Ask:

- Does this belief make people more afraid — or more free?

- Does it rely on threat to motivate change, or does it invite transformation through love?

- Does it require certainty and silence, or does it allow honesty and growth?

- Does it shrink people's humanity, or help them become more fully themselves?

- Does it produce compliance — or cultivate maturity?

- Does it heal desire, or merely control behaviour?

- Does it centralise control, or strengthen trust and relationship?

Then ask one final, grounding question:

- When this belief is lived out over time, does it make people more like Jesus —
  or merely more manageable?

These questions do not bypass Scripture.
They honour Scripture by taking Jesus seriously as its centre.

Fear-based frameworks can appear faithful while quietly producing anxiety, shame, and dependence.
Union-based faith produces freedom, resilience, honesty, and love — even when answers are incomplete.

Discernment is not about choosing the *safest* belief.
It is about choosing the belief that aligns with the character of Christ and the fruit of the Spirit.

APPENDIX B — WHEN THIS THEOLOGY IS MISUNDERSTOOD

Common Objections, Gently Addressed

This theology often sounds unfamiliar not because it is new,
but because it removes fear from places where fear has long been normalised.

The questions below are not signs of bad faith.
They are the kinds of questions people ask when long-held assumptions are being gently undone.

"Isn't this dangerous?"

Only if love is dangerous.

Fear has never produced lasting transformation.
It has produced compliance, silence, and anxiety.

Jesus consistently entrusted people with freedom —
even when they misused it, misunderstood Him, or walked away.

He did not manage behaviour through threat.
He revealed truth and trusted love to do its work.

The danger is not freedom.
The danger is teaching people that God must be feared in order to be trusted.

"Does this remove accountability?"

No.
It relocates accountability from fear to truth.

Fear-based accountability asks:
"What will happen to me if I don't comply?"

Love-based accountability asks:
"Is this aligned with what is true — about God, about myself, and about the world I am participating in?"

This does not weaken accountability.
It deepens it.

Fear can produce short-term compliance.
It cannot produce ownership.

Jesus consistently holds people responsible —
but He does so by restoring clarity, not by inducing terror.

He tells the truth about actions, consequences, and harm.
He names what is misaligned.
He exposes what destroys life.

But He does not outsource responsibility to fear.

Responsibility grounded in truth goes deeper than responsibility enforced by threat.
Threat manages behaviour.
Truth transforms desire.

This theology does not say, *"Nothing matters."*
It says, *"Everything matters — because reality matters."*

Actions still have consequences.
Harm still requires repair.
Deception still collapses under light.

The difference is this:
accountability is no longer about avoiding punishment —
it is about facing reality and becoming whole.

That is not less serious.
It is more.

"Is this moral relativism?"

No.
It removes fear — not truth.

Moral relativism says there *is* no objective reality to align with.
This theology says the opposite: **reality is real, structured, and truthful — and it cannot be negotiated.**

Sin is not subjective.
Harm is not imaginary.
Misalignment still damages people, relationships, and communities.

What changes is not *whether* things matter, but *why* they matter.

Fear-based systems enforce morality by threat:
"Obey, or suffer."

Jesus grounds morality in reality:
"This is how life actually works."

Truth is not optional.
Actions still carry consequences.
Deception still collapses under light.
What destroys life remains destructive, no matter how sincerely it is justified.

This theology does not loosen moral clarity.
It sharpens it.

Right and wrong are not decided by preference or culture.
They are revealed by what aligns with love, produces life, and reflects reality as Jesus embodies it.

Relativism avoids judgment by denying truth.
Jesus reveals judgment by **exposing truth**.

Fear may control behaviour.
Truth forms conscience.

This is not a softer ethic.
It is a deeper one.

"Does this minimise sin?"

No.
It takes sin seriously enough to name it accurately.

Sin is not legal guilt to be punished.
It is blindness, misbelief, and lost identity that must be healed.

Fear treats sin as rebellion to crush.
Jesus treats sin as deception to expose and restore.

This does not excuse harm.
It names its true source — and therefore its true cure.

"What about Paul's thorn in the flesh?"

Paul's "thorn in the flesh" is often treated as proof that God uses suffering, illness, or affliction to teach humility or withhold healing.

The text does not require that conclusion.

First, Paul never identifies the thorn as sickness.
He describes it as *"a messenger of Satan"* — language he consistently uses elsewhere for opposition, persecution, or spiritual harassment, not divine instruction.

Second, the thorn is not framed as God teaching Paul through pain.
It is framed as something God does **not remove**, while simultaneously revealing a deeper truth about strength, dependence, and identity.

Paul does not conclude, *"God gave me this to make me holy."*
He concludes, *"God's grace is sufficient, and His power is revealed in weakness."*

That is a crucial distinction.

The passage does not say suffering is good.
It says God is faithful **within** unresolved suffering.

Paul is not being formed by pain itself.
He is being formed by **trust** in the midst of limitation.

Nothing in this text suggests that God prefers sickness, withholds healing to teach lessons, or contradicts the healing posture revealed in Jesus.

It simply acknowledges a reality the rest of Scripture also affirms:
God does not abandon people when healing is delayed, partial, or mysterious.

The thorn does not redefine God's character.
It reveals God's presence when outcomes are unresolved.

Paul's experience must be interpreted **in light of Jesus**, not used to reinterpret Jesus away.

"Isn't this just permissive?"

No.
Permissiveness avoids truth to keep peace.

This theology insists on truth —
but without coercion, humiliation, or threat.

Jesus does not avoid confrontation.
He avoids domination.

Love is not permissive.
It is demanding in a deeper way —
because it calls people into freedom, not compliance.

"Is this universalism?"

This is **Christ-centred hope**, rooted in Scripture and early Christianity.

It affirms:

- the seriousness of sin

- the reality of judgment

- the necessity of repentance

- the centrality of Christ

It also affirms that God's justice is restorative, that His purposes are not thwarted by death, and that love completes what it begins.

This is not denial of consequence.
It is confidence in the faithfulness of God.

Common Objections About Hell

"Doesn't Jesus clearly teach eternal punishment?"

Jesus clearly teaches judgment.
He does not teach abandonment.

The confusion comes from reading Jesus' warnings through later fear-based frameworks rather than through His own life, language, and purpose.

Jesus uses urgent, confrontational imagery because what He is addressing is serious. He is not casual about destruction, hypocrisy, or self-deception. But seriousness does not require retribution — and urgency does not require hopelessness.

When Jesus speaks of *fire*, *outer darkness*, or *weeping and gnashing of teeth*, He is not describing a torture chamber God maintains forever. He is describing what happens when truth collides with resistance — when reality presses in on what refuses to let go of illusion.

Jesus' warnings function as interventions, not threats of abandonment.

They are meant to stop trajectories that destroy life — not to declare that God has given up on people forever.

"What about Matthew 25 — 'eternal punishment'?"

Matthew 25 is often treated as a mic-drop verse, but only if one assumption goes unexamined.

The Greek word translated *eternal* is aiōnios, which means *belonging to an age*, *age-shaped*, or *pertaining to a divine order* — not endless duration by default.

The contrast in Matthew 25 is not between:

> endless torture vs endless bliss

It is between:

> *life aligned with the Kingdom
> and judgment that confronts what resists it*

The punishment Jesus describes is real, weighty, and serious — but Scripture never requires us to read it as endless conscious torment sustained by God forever.

Especially when Scripture itself goes on to say:

- death is destroyed

- all things are made new

- God becomes "all in all"

Judgment belongs to the age of correction.
Life belongs to the age of God.

The Bible never says judgment outlasts God's purpose to heal.

"If hell is restorative, is it really judgment?"

Yes — more so than retribution ever was.

Retributive punishment ends the conversation.
Restorative judgment forces truth into the open.

Hell, as revealed through Jesus, is not the suspension of justice — it is justice without hatred, justice without abandonment, justice without denial.

Fire does not negotiate.
Light does not flatter.
Truth does not soften itself to avoid discomfort.

Restorative judgment is not lenient.
It is exacting — because it refuses illusion.

It burns away:

- false identity

- self-deception

- domination

- violence

- religious hypocrisy

What survives is what is real.

That is judgment.

"Doesn't this make hell sound less serious?"

No.
It makes it more serious.

Fear-based hell theology makes suffering meaningless and endless.
Jesus' vision makes suffering purposeful — because it is aimed at healing.

Endless punishment would mean evil is preserved forever.
Jesus comes to destroy the works of the devil, not maintain them.

Hell is not trivial.
It is severe mercy.

The seriousness of hell is not measured by how long pain lasts —
but by how completely lies are undone.

"If hell isn't final, why would anyone change?"

This question reveals more than it intends.

If the only reason to turn toward God is fear of endless punishment, then fear — not love — has become the centre of faith.

Jesus never motivates repentance that way.

People change when:

- truth becomes unavoidable

- love becomes credible

- illusion stops working

Fear can force compliance.
It cannot heal desire.

Jesus trusts truth and love to do what threat never could.

"So does everyone get saved automatically?"

No one is saved *automatically*.

Salvation is not a bypass.
It is an encounter.

Union is real — but resistance is also real.
Judgment is real.
Fire is real.
Transformation is real.

What this theology refuses to accept is that death, sin, or resistance are stronger than God's commitment to heal.

Grace is not fragile.
Love does not fail halfway through its work.

Hope in restoration is not denial of judgment.
It is confidence in God.

"Why does this feel so threatening if it's true?"

"Because fear has been normalised.

When fear is removed, truth initially feels unsafe — not because it is false, but because control has lost its leverage.

This teaching does not remove accountability.
It removes terror.

It does not minimise judgment.
It reveals its purpose.

And it does not deny hell.
It refuses to turn hell into God's final word.

Jesus is the final word.

"What about holiness?"

Holiness was never fear-based behaviour management.

Holiness is shared life with God —
a life that reshapes desire, not merely restrains action.

Jesus does not make people holy by threatening them.
He makes them holy by making them whole.

Holiness grows where love is trusted
and identity is restored.

"Does this reject Scripture?"

No.
It takes Scripture seriously enough to read it through Jesus.

Jesus does not become true because Scripture says so.
Scripture becomes clear because Jesus reveals God.

This is not a low view of the Bible.
It is a Jesus-centred one.

"What if people misuse this freedom?"

Some will.

Jesus knew that — and chose love anyway.

The possibility of misuse does not negate the goodness of freedom.
It reveals the cost God is willing to bear for real relationship.

God does not remove freedom to prevent failure.
He stays present to redeem it.

"Why does this feel so unfamiliar?"

Because fear has been normalised.

When fear is removed,
love can initially feel unsafe —
not because it is dangerous,
but because it asks for trust rather than control.

Unfamiliar does not mean unfaithful.

In Closing

This theology is not an escape from truth.
It is a return to the truth revealed in Jesus.

If it feels unsettling,
that may not be because it is wrong —
but because fear is loosening its grip.

And when fear loosens,
what often remains is not chaos,
but clarity, compassion, and Christ.

APPENDIX C — A PASTORAL GUIDE FOR THOSE DECONSTRUCTING

Reassurance Without Rushing Reconstruction

If fear is leaving and questions are rising,
something important is happening.

You are not broken.
You are not faithless.
You are not alone.

For many, deconstruction begins not with doubt,
but with honesty finally becoming unavoidable.

Something no longer fits.
Something no longer feels true, safe, or life-giving.
And pretending costs more than questioning.

This is not failure.
It is discernment awakening.

God is not standing at the edge of your questions,
waiting for you to resolve them correctly.

He is already present inside them —
patient, non-anxious, and near.

What to Expect (So You Don't Panic)

Deconstruction often includes:

- emotional swings — relief one day, grief the next
- moments of clarity followed by confusion
- anger at manipulation alongside longing for what once felt secure
- loneliness, even when surrounded by people
- fear that you are "going too far"

None of these mean you are doing something wrong.

When fear loosens its grip,
the nervous system needs time to recalibrate.

This is not spiritual danger.
It is recovery.

What to Hold Onto (Practically, Not Abstractly)

Hold onto Jesus.
Not as a system to defend,
but as a person to keep returning to.

Read the Gospels slowly.
Pay attention to how Jesus treats people —
especially the confused, the wounded, and the questioning.

If your faith still looks like Jesus,
you are not lost.

Hold onto love.
When unsure what to believe,
choose the most loving action available.

Love is not vague.
It looks like kindness, protection of the vulnerable,
honesty without cruelty, and refusal to harm.

You will not drift away from God by choosing love.

Hold onto honesty.
Say what is actually true.

"I don't know."
"I'm angry."
"I'm grieving."
"I'm afraid."

God does not require emotional editing.
Honesty is not disloyalty — it is relationship.

Hold onto humility.
You are allowed to hold convictions loosely.
You are allowed to change your mind.
You are allowed to be wrong without collapsing.

Humility keeps the soul open and safe.

What to Let Go Of (So Healing Isn't Undone)

Let go of fear-based urgency.
You do not need to land somewhere quickly.
God is not in a hurry.

Pressure to "figure it all out"
is usually fear trying to regain control.

Let go of performative certainty.
You do not owe anyone a finished theology.
You do not need to sound confident to be faithful.

Faith is not proven by certainty.
It is revealed by trust.

Let go of spiritual superiority.
Awakening is not elevation above others.
It is deepening into compassion.

If your new insights make you less gentle,
something has gone wrong.

How to Care for Yourself in This Season

- Find at least one safe person who does not rush you

- Limit exposure to voices that shame or threaten

- Take breaks from constant theological consumption

- Ground yourself in practices that calm your body, not just your mind

- Remember that healing is not linear

You are allowed to rest.
You are allowed to pause.
You are allowed to rebuild slowly — or not at all for a while.

A Word About Truth

You are not losing truth.
You are losing fear.

Truth does not need anxiety to survive.
It does not require threat, pressure, or suppression.

What remains after fear loosens
is often simpler, truer, and more life-giving
than what came before.

Deconstruction does not mean God is gone.
It often means false images of God are falling away.

And when they do,
many discover that what remains
is not emptiness —
but presence.

In Closing

You are not being tested.
You are not on probation.
You are not falling away.

You are learning to trust without fear.

And God is not watching from a distance.
He is walking with you —
inside the questions,
inside the grief,
inside the slow return to safety.

Take your time.

Love is not in a hurry.

APPENDIX D — THE KINGDOM CREED

A Jesus-Shaped Invitation Into Awakening

This is not a formula.
It is a response to reality already revealed in Christ.

Jesus,
You reveal the Father's heart and my true identity.
I awaken to Your life, Your Spirit, and Your truth.
Open my eyes to our union.
Heal me, transform me, restore me.
I choose Your way of love, abundance, and joy.
Let Your Kingdom fill my life — now and forever.
Amen.

This prayer does not replace faith — it expresses it.

APPENDIX E — THE WITNESS OF THE EARLY CHURCH

1. THE EARLY CHURCH READ SCRIPTURE THROUGH JESUS

The earliest Christians did not treat Scripture as a flat rulebook or a self-interpreting legal code.
They understood Scripture as:

- a sacred story

- a progressive revelation

- a witness pointing toward Christ

Jesus Himself was the interpretive key.

Origen repeatedly emphasised that the purpose of Scripture was not the accumulation of information about God, but formation in Christ and participation in divine life.[1]

For many early Christian teachers, the Gospels were not simply one set of texts among others. They were the lens through which everything else was read.

When Old Testament portrayals of God appeared violent, coercive, or vengeful, early theologians — particularly in the Greek tradition — did not assume Jesus needed correction. They assumed human understanding was still maturing.

This Jesus-first reading of Scripture is not a modern innovation.
It is one of the earliest Christian hermeneutical instincts.

---

2. SALVATION AS HEALING, NOT LEGAL ACQUITTAL

In much early Christian theology, the controlling metaphor for salvation was medicine, not the courtroom.

Sin was not primarily framed as a legal problem requiring punishment, but as a condition requiring healing. Humanity was understood as wounded, disoriented, and diminished — not merely guilty.

Sin was commonly described as:

- sickness

- blindness

- deformation of desire

- participation in unreality

Salvation, therefore, was understood as:

- healing

- illumination

- restoration

- re-formation into Christlikeness

"The glory of God is a human being fully alive."
— Irenaeus of Lyons[2]

Christ was repeatedly described as:

- the Physician

- the Light

- the Healer of the soul

- the Restorer of the divine image

The central question was not,
"How can God punish sin and still be just?"
but,
"What has gone wrong in humanity — and how does God heal it without violating human nature?"

Legal categories of guilt, punishment, and satisfaction were present but not controlling in early Christianity. They become dominant much later, particularly in the medieval Western Church, shaped by Roman legal frameworks and feudal concepts of justice.

For many early Christians, salvation was primarily ontological and participatory:

- humanity sharing in Christ's life

- the image of God being restored

- desire being healed

- truth displacing illusion

God was not imagined as needing persuasion to forgive.
God was already acting as the healer.

To be saved was to be made whole.

---

3. SIN AS LOSS OF ALIGNMENT, NOT INHERITED LEGAL GUILT

Early Christian writers frequently described sin as:

- misalignment

- loss of likeness

- participation in illusion

- turning away from life

"Evil has no substance of its own; it is the absence of good."
— Gregory of Nyssa[3]

Sin was not primarily an offense against God's honour.
It was a tragedy for humanity.

This is why repentance (*metanoia*) was understood not as terror-driven remorse, but as:

- awakening

- reorientation

- return to truth

- restoration of vision

This understanding closely mirrors Jesus' own teaching.

4. JUDGMENT AS PURIFICATION, NOT RETRIBUTION

Early Christian theology did not deny judgment.
But many early teachers rejected retributive punishment as God's final posture.

Judgment was understood as:

- the revelation of truth

- the exposure of illusion

- the purification of the soul

- a painful but healing confrontation with reality

"God's fire is not a fire that destroys, but one that purifies."
— Clement of Alexandria[4]

Fire was consistently interpreted as:

- refining

- corrective

- medicinal

- oriented toward restoration

Judgment was not something love suspends.
It was something love does.

---

5. HELL AS REAL, SERIOUS — AND TEMPORAL

One of the most contested areas of early Christian theology concerns hell.

While views varied, a significant and respected stream of early Christian thought — including figures foundational to orthodoxy — understood hell as:

- real
- serious
- painful
- corrective
- temporal

"God's punishments are remedial, not retributive."
— Origen[1]

"The aim of punishment is the healing of the soul."
— Gregory of Nyssa[3]

Gregory of Nyssa:

- was a champion of Nicene orthodoxy

- helped shape Trinitarian theology

- was never condemned as a heretic

- clearly articulated a vision of ultimate restoration in which evil is finally undone and God becomes "all in all"

The claim that eternal conscious torment represented the only orthodox position in the early Church is historically difficult to sustain, given the diversity of respected theological voices in the first centuries.

6. APOKATASTASIS — THE RESTORATION OF ALL THINGS

The term *apokatastasis* comes directly from Scripture:

"Until the time for the restoration of all things."
— Acts 3:21

For many early Christians, this was not speculative theology. It flowed naturally from convictions that:

- God is love

- Christ has defeated death

- God's purposes do not fail

- judgment serves healing, not opposition to love

"God will be 'all in all' when no being remains outside the range of goodness."
— Gregory of Nyssa, *On the Soul and the Resurrection*[3]

Universal restoration was not fringe.
It was one respected stream among several within early Christianity — particularly in the Greek East.

This hope was not universal nor uncontested in early Christianity, but it was neither marginal nor heretical in the centuries before later doctrinal consolidations.

---

7. THE AUGUSTINIAN TURN — AND WHY IT MATTERS

The shift toward fear-based frameworks was gradual, contextual, and contested.

Eternal conscious torment, penal substitution, and juridical models of salvation do not dominate the earliest centuries of Christianity. They emerge later, especially in the Western Church, shaped by new cultural, philosophical, and political pressures.

Augustine of Hippo (4th–5th century) played a pivotal role in this transition. His immense influence meant that his interpretations — particularly regarding sin, grace, and judgment — became foundational in the West, even where they diverged from earlier Greek traditions.

Several factors shaped this turn:

- Latin translation choices, especially rendering *aiōnios* as *aeternus* (endless duration), contributing to a hardening of judgment language beyond what the Greek necessarily requires[5]

- Roman legal frameworks, which recast sin as crime rather than sickness

- Platonic assumptions about inherent immortality of the soul

- The pastoral use of fear as a tool for social cohesion in a post-imperial Church

This was not theological malice.
It was theological context.

And what is contextual can be examined.

---

8. RETRIEVAL, NOT REVISION

This manuscript does not discard tradition.
It distinguishes tradition.

It stands within:

- Jesus' teaching

- apostolic proclamation

- early Christian imagination

- Greek patristic theology

- a restorative vision of God

Some traditions heal.
Some distort.

The early Church reminds us that:

- love precedes law

- union precedes obedience

- healing precedes judgment

- restoration precedes exclusion

This is not a soft gospel.
It is a stronger one.

CONCLUDING STATEMENT

Many early Christian teachers were not afraid of love winning.

They trusted that:

- God is good

- Christ is victorious

- truth heals

- love endures

- restoration is the final word

This manuscript does not invent a new Christianity.
It listens again to an old one —
before fear was mistaken for faith.

ENDNOTES (Appendix E)

1. Origen, *De Principiis*; *Homilies on Jeremiah*. See his consistent emphasis on Scripture as formative rather than merely

informational across his exegetical works.

2. Irenaeus, *Against Heresies*, IV.20.7.

3. Gregory of Nyssa, *On the Soul and the Resurrection*; see also *The Great Catechism*.

4. Clement of Alexandria, *Stromata*, esp. Book VII.

5. On *aiōnios* and translation issues, see discussions in early Greek patristic usage and later Latin renderings (e.g., *aeternus*), including debates noted in patristic scholarship and lexical studies of Second Temple and early Christian Greek.

APPENDIX F — Fear-Based Mission vs Witness-Based Mission

This appendix does not introduce new ideas.
It names, side-by-side, the *practical outcomes* of two very different mission postures that often use the same Christian language.

Only one reflects the posture of Jesus.

Fear-Based Mission

Begins with the assumption that God is distant, absent, or withheld

Treats people as problems to be fixed or dangers to be neutralised

Is driven by urgency rooted in threat

Measures success by decisions, numbers, or compliance

Uses pressure, persuasion, or emotional leverage

Frames the Gospel primarily as a warning to escape

Relates to people as projects rather than persons

Produces anxiety, performative faith, and shallow conversion

Teaches people to obey God out of fear of consequences

Often leaves people feeling coerced, ashamed, or spiritually unsafe

Fear-based mission may secure responses —
but it cannot form trust, freedom, or love.

Witness-Based Mission

Begins with the reality that God is already present and active

Treats people as image-bearers already held within God's care

Is driven by love, patience, and trust in the Spirit

Measures faithfulness by truthfulness, presence, and formation

Uses honesty, invitation, and embodied love

Frames the Gospel as good news to awaken to

Relates to people as neighbours, not targets

Produces curiosity, trust, and lasting transformation

Teaches people to respond to God because love has made it safe

Leaves people more free, grounded, and alive

Witness-based mission does not force belief —
it reveals reality and trusts truth to do its work.

The Difference at the Core

Fear-based mission asks:
"How do we get people to respond?"

Witness-based mission asks:
"How do we tell the truth about what we have seen?"

Fear tries to manage outcomes.
Love bears witness and releases control.

Jesus does not commission fear as a method.
He commissions His followers to testify —
with their words, their lives, and their love —
to a Kingdom already breaking in.

In Short

Fear produces compliance.
Witness produces trust.

Fear makes God the threat.
Witness reveals God as the gift.

Mission does not require urgency driven by fear —
only faithfulness grounded in love.

FINAL WORD TO THE READER

This book does not ask you to agree with everything you have read.
It asks you to breathe again.

If something here brought clarity, keep it.
If something unsettled you, hold it gently.
If something felt unfamiliar, stay curious rather than defensive.

Jesus does not need defending.
He needs revealing.

You are not required to hurry.
Truth does not rush.
Love does not panic.

If fear loosened its grip as you read, that matters.
If shame lost authority, that matters.
If God felt safer, closer, or more human, that matters.

Nothing honest separates you from God.
Nothing sincere puts you at risk.
Nothing true requires fear to survive.

You are not being measured.
You are not being tested.
You are not behind.

Wherever love grows, the Kingdom is already near.
Wherever truth heals, Christ is present.
Wherever fear loses power, resurrection is at work.

Walk gently.
Live awake.
Trust what produces life.

And remember this:

Jesus has always been better than we were told.

Thank you for reading.

If this book resonated with you, even in a small way, a short review would mean more than you might realise. Reviews help thoughtful books find thoughtful readers.

You can leave a review here:

United States:
https://www.amazon.com/review/create-review?asin=0646734814

Australia:
https://www.amazon.com.au/review/create-review?asin=0646734814

If you'd like to explore more writing, essays, or future books, you can find me at:
https://johnfaulknerauthor.com

www.ingramcontent.com/pod-product-compliance
Lightning Source LLC
Chambersburg PA
CBHW021147160426
43194CB00007B/725